Decoding the TOEFL® iBT

Actual Test

SPEAKING 1

INTRODUCTION

For many learners of English, the TOEFL® iBT will be the most important standardized test they ever take. Unfortunately for a large number of these individuals, the material covered on the TOEFL® iBT remains a mystery to them, so they are unable to do well on the test. We hope that by using the *Decoding the TOEFL® iBT* series, individuals who take the TOEFL® iBT will be able to excel on the test and, in the process of using the book, may unravel the mysteries of the test and therefore make the material covered on the TOEFL® iBT more familiar to themselves.

The TOEFL® iBT covers the four main skills that a person must learn when studying any foreign language: reading, listening, speaking, and writing. The *Decoding the TOEFL® iBT* series contains books that cover all four of these skills. The *Decoding the TOEFL® iBT* series contains books with three separate levels for all four of the topics, and it also contains *Decoding the TOEFL® iBT Actual Test* books. These books contain several actual tests that learners can utilize to help them become better prepared to take the TOEFL® iBT. This book, *Decoding the TOEFL® iBT Actual Test Speaking 1*, covers the speaking aspect of the test and includes both independent and integrated tasks that are arranged in the same format as the TOEFL® iBT. Finally, the TOEFL® iBT underwent a number of changes in August 2019. This book—and the others in the series—takes those changes into account and incorporates them in the texts and questions, so readers of this second edition can be assured that they have up-to-date knowledge of the test.

Decoding the TOEFL® iBT Actual Test Speaking 1 can be used by learners who are taking classes and also by individuals who are studying by themselves. It contains a total of twenty full-length speaking actual tests. Each actual test contains one independent task (question 1) and three integrated tasks (questions 2-4). All of the passages, conversations, and lectures that are used in the tasks are the same length and have the same difficulty levels as those found on the TOEFL® iBT. Individuals who use *Decoding the TOEFL® iBT Actual Test Speaking 1* will therefore be able to prepare themselves not only to take the TOEFL® iBT but also to perform well on the test.

We hope that everyone who uses *Decoding the TOEFL® iBT Actual Test Speaking 1* will be able to become more familiar with the TOEFL® iBT and will additionally improve his or her score on the test. As the title of the book implies, we hope that learners can use it to crack the code on the TOEFL® iBT, to make the test itself less mysterious and confusing, and to get the highest score possible. Finally, we hope that both learners and instructors can use this book to its full potential. We wish all of you the best of luck as you study English and prepare for the TOEFL® iBT, and we hope that *Decoding the TOEFL® iBT Actual Test Speaking 1* can provide you with assistance during the course of your studies.

Michael A. Putlack
Stephen Poirier
Tony Covello

TABLE
OF
CONTENTS

ABOUT THE TOEFL® iBT SPEAKING SECTION

How the Section Is Organized

The Speaking section is the third part of the TOEFL® iBT and consists of four questions. Question 1 is called the Independent Speaking Task and asks test takers to speak about a familiar topic. The other questions, questions 2-4, are called the Integrated Speaking Tasks. These tasks require test takers to integrate their speaking skills with other language skills such as listening and reading skills.

For each of the four questions, test takers are given preparation time and response time. During the preparation time, test takers can write down brief notes about how they will organize their responses. The preparation time ranges from 15 to 30 seconds, and the response time is either 45 or 60 seconds. The spoken responses are recorded and sent to be scored by raters. The raters evaluate responses based on three criteria: Delivery (how clear your speech is), Language Use (how effectively you use grammar and vocabulary to convey your ideas), and Topic Development (how fully you answer the question and how coherently you present your ideas).

Changes in the Speaking Section

The Speaking section is the section that has gone through the most drastic changes. Two question types – Questions 1 and 5 on the old test – have been removed. Therefore, the total number of questions has become four instead of six. Accordingly, the time allotted for the Speaking section has been reduced from 20 minutes to 17 minutes. However, the remaining questions have no changes, and the preparation times and the response times remain the same.

Question Types

TYPE 1 Independent Speaking Task: Question 1

The first question asks test takers to speak about a familiar topic. It is necessary for test takers to include specific examples and details in their response. After the question is presented, test takers are given 15 seconds to prepare their response and 45 seconds to speak.

Question 1 asks test takers to make a personal choice between two possible opinions, actions, or situations. In addition, on recent tests, test takers are sometimes given three options from which to choose, and they may be asked to speak about both the advantages and the disadvantages of a particular topic. Test takers are required to explain their choice by providing reasons and details. Topics for this question include everyday issues of general interest to test takers. For example, the question may ask about a preference between studying at home and studying at the library, a preference between living in a dormitory and living in an off-campus apartment, or a preference between a class with a lot of discussion and one without discussion.

ABOUT THE
TOEFL® iBT
SPEAKING SECTION

TYPE 2 **Integrated Speaking Tasks** (Reading, Listening, and Speaking): **Questions 2 and 3**

The second and third questions require test takers to integrate different language skills. Test takers are first presented with a short reading passage. The time given for reading is 45-50 seconds. After that, test takers will listen to a conversation or a lecture which is related to information presented in the reading passage. They need to organize their response by using information from both the reading passage and the conversation or lecture. For these questions, test takers are given 30 seconds to prepare their response and 60 seconds to speak.

Question 2 concerns a topic of campus-related interest, but it does not require prior firsthand experience of college or university life in North America to understand the topic. The reading passage is usually between 75 and 100 words long. It may be an announcement, letter, or article regarding a policy, rule, or future plan of a college or university. It can also be related to campus facilities or the quality of life on campus. After reading the passage, test takers will listen to two speakers discuss the topic presented in the reading passage. Typically, one of the two speakers shows a strong opinion about the topic. On recent tests, however, speakers have shown mixed feelings about the topic, so they like it yet also dislike some aspect of it. Test takers need to summarize the speaker's opinion and the reasons for holding it.

In Question 3, test takers will read a short passage about an academic subject and then listen to a professor lecture about that subject. The question requires test takers to relate the reading passage and the lecture. Topics for this question can be drawn from a variety of fields, including life science, social science, physical science, and the humanities. However, the question does not require prior knowledge of any particular field.

TYPE 3 **Integrated Speaking Tasks** (Listening and Speaking): **Question 4**

The last question presents only a listening passage—a lecture—and not a reading passage. Test takers need to respond based on what they hear. They are given 20 seconds to prepare their response and 60 seconds to speak.

For Question 4, test takers will listen to a lecture about an academic topic. As in Question 3, topics for this question can be drawn from a variety of fields, including life science, social science, physical science, and the humanities. Again, no prior knowledge is necessary to understand the lecture. After hearing the lecture, test takers are asked to summarize the lecture and to explain how the examples are connected with the overall topic.

Actual Test

01

Speaking Section Directions

 Make sure your headset is on.

This section measures your ability to speak about a variety of topics. You will answer four questions by speaking into the microphone. Answer as completely as possible.

In the first question, you will speak about a familiar topic. Your response will be scored on your ability to speak clearly and coherently.

In the next two questions, you will first read a short reading passage. This passage will go away, and you will then listen to a talk on the same topic. You will be asked about the information you have read and heard. You will need to combine information from the reading passage and the talk to provide a complete answer. Your response will be scored on your ability to speak clearly and coherently and how accurately you convey information about what you read and heard.

In the last question, you will listen to part of a lecture. You will be asked about what you have heard. Your response will be scored on your ability to speak clearly and coherently and how accurately you convey information about what you heard.

You may take notes while you read and while you listen to the conversations and lectures. You may use your notes to help prepare your response.

Listen carefully to the directions for each question. The directions will not be written on the screen.

For each question, you will be given a short time to prepare your response (15 to 30 seconds, depending on the question). A clock will show how much preparation time is remaining. When the preparation time is up, you will be told to begin your response. A clock will show how much response time is remaining. A message will appear on the screen when the response time has ended.

AT01-01

A school has just received a big donation. In which of the following ways should it spend the money?

- **By building a library that students can use to read books and to study in**
- **By constructing a gym that students can play sports and exercise in**

Use details and examples to explain your answer.

PREPARATION TIME
00:00:15

RESPONSE TIME
00:00:45

🎧 AT01-02

New Requirement for Pre-Med Students

Beginning next year, all juniors pursuing pre-med studies must complete a two-month internship at City Hospital. The purpose of this internship will be to enable students to decide whether they would like to attend medical school upon graduating. All pre-med students who apply to do the internship will be approved by City Hospital provided that they are in good academic standing with the school. The internships will be done during summer vacation to avoid interfering with students' regular schoolwork. For more information, contact Ms. Cindy Summers at extension 506.

The woman expresses her opinion about the announcement by the Biology Department. Explain her opinion and the reasons she gives for holding that opinion.

PREPARATION TIME
00:00:30

RESPONSE TIME
00:00:60

🎧 AT01-03

Reactance

There are times when one person may place a restriction on the behavior of another individual. When a rule limiting a person's behavior or actions is implemented, the affected person often feels that his or her freedom has been lessened. The person is then more likely to engage in the behavior or action that has been restricted. This type of behavior is known as reactance. It is a result of an affected individual demonstrating that he or she still possesses the free will and ability to make decisions of his or her own.

The professor talks about her son and daughter. Explain how their actions are related to reactance.

PREPARATION TIME
00:00:30

RESPONSE TIME
00:00:60

AT01-04

Using points and examples from the talk, explain how people are trying to reduce the amount of carbon dioxide in the atmosphere.

PREPARATION TIME
00:00:20

RESPONSE TIME
00:00:60

Actual Test

02

Speaking Section Directions

 Make sure your headset is on.

This section measures your ability to speak about a variety of topics. You will answer four questions by speaking into the microphone. Answer as completely as possible.

In the first question, you will speak about a familiar topic. Your response will be scored on your ability to speak clearly and coherently.

In the next two questions, you will first read a short reading passage. This passage will go away, and you will then listen to a talk on the same topic. You will be asked about the information you have read and heard. You will need to combine information from the reading passage and the talk to provide a complete answer. Your response will be scored on your ability to speak clearly and coherently and how accurately you convey information about what you read and heard.

In the last question, you will listen to part of a lecture. You will be asked about what you have heard. Your response will be scored on your ability to speak clearly and coherently and how accurately you convey information about what you heard.

You may take notes while you read and while you listen to the conversations and lectures. You may use your notes to help prepare your response.

Listen carefully to the directions for each question. The directions will not be written on the screen.

For each question, you will be given a short time to prepare your response (15 to 30 seconds, depending on the question). A clock will show how much preparation time is remaining. When the preparation time is up, you will be told to begin your response. A clock will show how much response time is remaining. A message will appear on the screen when the response time has ended.

🎧 CD 02-01

Which do you prefer, playing individual sports or team sports? Use details and examples to explain your answer.

PREPARATION TIME
00:00:15

RESPONSE TIME
00:00:45

🎧 AT02-02

Changes to Be Made in Tomorrow's Elections

All students should be aware that there are two changes in tomorrow's student council elections. First of all, there will be no voting in the student library as the librarians have claimed that voting there would be too noisy. As a result, voting will only be permitted in the student center and at the student cafeteria. The second change concerns the student cafeteria. Voting there will end at 8 P.M. rather than at 9 P.M. since the cafeteria regularly closes at eight. Those students wishing to vote between eight and nine must do so at the student center.

The man expresses his opinion about the article in the school newspaper. Explain his opinion and the reasons he gives for holding that opinion.

PREPARATION TIME
00:00:30

RESPONSE TIME
00:00:60

16

AT02-03

Animal Warning Coloration

Prey animals employ a variety of methods, including running and hiding, to avoid being caught by predators. Yet some animals do not hide but instead stand out. This is often accomplished through the method known as warning coloration. Animals utilizing warning coloration have brightly colored fur or skin. They are typically blue, purple, white, orange, red, or yellow in color. Many of these animals have lethal poison or venom. Predators that see brightly colored animals almost always avoid them. That is particularly true if the predators have had prior negative experiences with similar-looking animals.

The professor talks about the poison dart frog and the skunk. Explain how their actions are related to animal warning coloration.

PREPARATION TIME
00:00:30

RESPONSE TIME
00:00:60

🎧 AT02-04

Using points and examples from the talk, explain two ways that natural arches are formed.

PREPARATION TIME
00:00:20

RESPONSE TIME
00:00:60

Actual Test

03

Speaking Section Directions

 Make sure your headset is on.

This section measures your ability to speak about a variety of topics. You will answer four questions by speaking into the microphone. Answer as completely as possible.

In the first question, you will speak about a familiar topic. Your response will be scored on your ability to speak clearly and coherently.

In the next two questions, you will first read a short reading passage. This passage will go away, and you will then listen to a talk on the same topic. You will be asked about the information you have read and heard. You will need to combine information from the reading passage and the talk to provide a complete answer. Your response will be scored on your ability to speak clearly and coherently and how accurately you convey information about what you read and heard.

In the last question, you will listen to part of a lecture. You will be asked about what you have heard. Your response will be scored on your ability to speak clearly and coherently and how accurately you convey information about what you heard.

You may take notes while you read and while you listen to the conversations and lectures. You may use your notes to help prepare your response.

Listen carefully to the directions for each question. The directions will not be written on the screen.

For each question, you will be given a short time to prepare your response (15 to 30 seconds, depending on the question). A clock will show how much preparation time is remaining. When the preparation time is up, you will be told to begin your response. A clock will show how much response time is remaining. A message will appear on the screen when the response time has ended.

AT03-01

Which is more important to you when deciding which university to attend, the location of the university or the price of tuition? Use details and examples to explain your answer.

PREPARATION TIME
00:00:15

RESPONSE TIME
00:00:45

AT03-02

Daily Notices to Be Sent by Email

Starting on Monday, September 2, the school administration will send email notices to students on a daily basis. These notices will concern various school events as well as academic and extracurricular activities. All notices will be sent to students' university-issued email addresses. Students should be sure to check their email every day as most of the information in these notices will not be reprinted in the school newspaper. Students with any questions or comments are encouraged to contact Jim Danner by calling 540-1020 or by visiting him in his office at 406 Winston Hall.

The woman expresses her opinion about the announcement by the school administration. Explain her opinion and the reasons she gives for holding that opinion.

PREPARATION TIME
00:00:30

RESPONSE TIME
00:00:60

🎧 AT03-03

Pheromones

Pheromones are chemical signals employed by all kinds of animals, including insects and mammals, for a wide variety of purposes. Among them are signals for mating, feeding, gathering, and following and warnings of danger. Each chemical signal is unique and is only understood by members of the same species. Pheromones are commonly scents that are either airborne or are sprayed onto objects where other members of the same species can detect them. Most pheromones are secreted by special glands in animals' bodies.

The professor talks about ants and honeybees. Explain how their actions are related to pheromones.

PREPARATION TIME
00:00:30

RESPONSE TIME
00:00:60

AT03-04

Using points and examples from the talk, explain the two main means of advertisements that are used.

PREPARATION TIME
00:00:20

RESPONSE TIME
00:00:60

Actual Test

04

Speaking Section Directions

 Make sure your headset is on.

This section measures your ability to speak about a variety of topics. You will answer four questions by speaking into the microphone. Answer as completely as possible.

In the first question, you will speak about a familiar topic. Your response will be scored on your ability to speak clearly and coherently.

In the next two questions, you will first read a short reading passage. This passage will go away, and you will then listen to a talk on the same topic. You will be asked about the information you have read and heard. You will need to combine information from the reading passage and the talk to provide a complete answer. Your response will be scored on your ability to speak clearly and coherently and how accurately you convey information about what you read and heard.

In the last question, you will listen to part of a lecture. You will be asked about what you have heard. Your response will be scored on your ability to speak clearly and coherently and how accurately you convey information about what you heard.

You may take notes while you read and while you listen to the conversations and lectures. You may use your notes to help prepare your response.

Listen carefully to the directions for each question. The directions will not be written on the screen.

For each question, you will be given a short time to prepare your response (15 to 30 seconds, depending on the question). A clock will show how much preparation time is remaining. When the preparation time is up, you will be told to begin your response. A clock will show how much response time is remaining. A message will appear on the screen when the response time has ended.

AT04-01

Do you agree or disagree with the following statement?

It is better to buy the newest goods instead of waiting for something better to come out later.

Use details and examples to explain your answer.

PREPARATION TIME
00:00:15

RESPONSE TIME
00:00:45

🎧 AT04-02

Kiosks Needed for Dormitories

Now that the final exam period is arriving soon, I have a suggestion for the administration. I would like for every dormitory on campus to have a kiosk selling food in its front lobby. Since students will be busy studying for their tests, they won't have time to go out for meals since doing so would disrupt their studies. Furthermore, by selling healthy foods such as fruits and vegetables at the kiosks, the school can enable students to avoid eating the junk food most of them commonly consume while they're studying. I hope the school administration considers my argument.

Janet Webber
Freshman

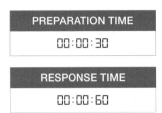

The man expresses his opinion about the letter to the editor in the school newspaper. Explain his opinion and the reasons he gives for holding that opinion.

PREPARATION TIME
00:00:30

RESPONSE TIME
00:00:60

🎧 AT04-03

Stress

Stress is an organism's response to a certain condition or outside stimulant known as a stressor. For humans, stress tends to make people feel as though they are being overwhelmed by various problems. Common stressors include health issues, money problems, work and school troubles, and relationship difficulties. The body's reaction to stress varies, but common responses include elevated blood pressure, an increased heart rate, nervousness, anxiety, sweating, a loss of appetite, and insomnia. People can ease their stress by talking about and then solving their problems. Exercising, sleeping well, and eating healthy meals additionally lessen stress.

The professor talks about one of her students. Explain how that student's actions are related to stress.

PREPARATION TIME
00:00:30

RESPONSE TIME
00:00:60

🎧 AT04-04

Using points and examples from the talk, explain how animals use venom to attack others and to defend themselves.

PREPARATION TIME
00:00:20

RESPONSE TIME
00:00:60

Actual Test

05

Speaking Section Directions

 Make sure your headset is on.

This section measures your ability to speak about a variety of topics. You will answer four questions by speaking into the microphone. Answer as completely as possible.

In the first question, you will speak about a familiar topic. Your response will be scored on your ability to speak clearly and coherently.

In the next two questions, you will first read a short reading passage. This passage will go away, and you will then listen to a talk on the same topic. You will be asked about the information you have read and heard. You will need to combine information from the reading passage and the talk to provide a complete answer. Your response will be scored on your ability to speak clearly and coherently and how accurately you convey information about what you read and heard.

In the last question, you will listen to part of a lecture. You will be asked about what you have heard. Your response will be scored on your ability to speak clearly and coherently and how accurately you convey information about what you heard.

You may take notes while you read and while you listen to the conversations and lectures. You may use your notes to help prepare your response.

Listen carefully to the directions for each question. The directions will not be written on the screen.

For each question, you will be given a short time to prepare your response (15 to 30 seconds, depending on the question). A clock will show how much preparation time is remaining. When the preparation time is up, you will be told to begin your response. A clock will show how much response time is remaining. A message will appear on the screen when the response time has ended.

AT05-01

Answer one of the following questions.

1   Some people prefer to spend time with their friends. Others prefer to spend time with their family members. Talk about the advantages and disadvantages of spending time with friends. Use details and examples to explain your answer.

2   Some people prefer to spend time with their friends. Others prefer to spend time with their family members. Talk about the advantages and disadvantages of spending time with family members. Use details and examples to explain your answer.

PREPARATION TIME
00:00:15

RESPONSE TIME
00:00:45

🎧 AT05-02

City College Receives Grant

City College is pleased to announce it has received an anonymous donation from a generous benefactor. The donation will be used to sponsor students who wish to visit various cultural spots in the city. These include all of the city's museums, art galleries, and zoos. Any student who wishes to visit one of these places may apply to the office of the dean of students for funding. Upon having his or her application accepted, the student may visit the cultural spot, pay the admission fee, and then receive a refund from the school upon submitting a receipt.

The woman expresses her opinion about the announcement by the dean of students. Explain her opinion and the reasons she gives for holding that opinion.

PREPARATION TIME
00:00:30

RESPONSE TIME
00:00:60

Dormancy

Some organisms are capable of reducing their metabolic activity a great degree. This is known as dormancy. An organism normally goes dormant when certain environmental factors cause it stress. As a result of this stress, the organism reduces its activity in order to save energy. Common stress factors include extremely high and low temperatures as well as overly arid conditions. Organisms that live in regions which experience these kinds of extremes can utilize their ability to become dormant for long periods of time to survive until conditions return to normal.

The professor talks about the lungfish. Explain how its actions are related to dormancy.

PREPARATION TIME
00:00:30

RESPONSE TIME
00:00:60

AT05-04

Using points and examples from the talk, explain how advertising can be considered wasteful.

PREPARATION TIME
00:00:20

RESPONSE TIME
00:00:60

Actual Test

06

Speaking Section Directions

 Make sure your headset is on.

This section measures your ability to speak about a variety of topics. You will answer four questions by speaking into the microphone. Answer as completely as possible.

In the first question, you will speak about a familiar topic. Your response will be scored on your ability to speak clearly and coherently.

In the next two questions, you will first read a short reading passage. This passage will go away, and you will then listen to a talk on the same topic. You will be asked about the information you have read and heard. You will need to combine information from the reading passage and the talk to provide a complete answer. Your response will be scored on your ability to speak clearly and coherently and how accurately you convey information about what you read and heard.

In the last question, you will listen to part of a lecture. You will be asked about what you have heard. Your response will be scored on your ability to speak clearly and coherently and how accurately you convey information about what you heard.

You may take notes while you read and while you listen to the conversations and lectures. You may use your notes to help prepare your response.

Listen carefully to the directions for each question. The directions will not be written on the screen.

For each question, you will be given a short time to prepare your response (15 to 30 seconds, depending on the question). A clock will show how much preparation time is remaining. When the preparation time is up, you will be told to begin your response. A clock will show how much response time is remaining. A message will appear on the screen when the response time has ended.

🎧 AT06-01

Do you agree or disagree with the following statement?

Young children should not own cell phones.

Use details and examples to explain your answer.

PREPARATION TIME
00:00:15

RESPONSE TIME
00:00:45

AT06-02

Changes to Bike Rental Program Necessary

I feel that the school's new bike rental program is highly beneficial to the student body. However, I would like to propose two suggestions that could improve the overall quality of the program. To begin with, the cost of hourly rentals should be reduced. Currently, the price is too great for many students to afford. If it were cheaper, more students would be able to rent bikes. Furthermore, a student should be able to borrow a bicycle by leaving a valid student ID card as a deposit. The current deposit fee of $30 is too high.

Eric Gordon

Sophomore

The man expresses his opinion about the letter to the editor in the school newspaper. Explain his opinion and the reasons he gives for holding that opinion.

PREPARATION TIME
00:00:30

RESPONSE TIME
00:00:60

AT06-03

Market Research

Companies become successful by selling as many products or services as possible. To accomplish that mission, they must attract customers. One ideal way to find new customers is to do market research. This normally involves the conducting of surveys, which can be done by mail, over the telephone, or on the Internet. The results provide companies with a good idea of what people want and what kinds of individuals are attracted to their products or services. By utilizing market research, companies can make changes to retain their current customers and to find new ones.

The professor talks about a national video and DVD retailer. Explain how its experience is related to market research.

PREPARATION TIME
00:00:30

RESPONSE TIME
00:00:60

AT06-04

Using points and examples from the talk, explain two ways in which fish float in the water.

PREPARATION TIME
00:00:20

RESPONSE TIME
00:00:60

Actual Test

07

Speaking Section Directions

 Make sure your headset is on.

This section measures your ability to speak about a variety of topics. You will answer four questions by speaking into the microphone. Answer as completely as possible.

In the first question, you will speak about a familiar topic. Your response will be scored on your ability to speak clearly and coherently.

In the next two questions, you will first read a short reading passage. This passage will go away, and you will then listen to a talk on the same topic. You will be asked about the information you have read and heard. You will need to combine information from the reading passage and the talk to provide a complete answer. Your response will be scored on your ability to speak clearly and coherently and how accurately you convey information about what you read and heard.

In the last question, you will listen to part of a lecture. You will be asked about what you have heard. Your response will be scored on your ability to speak clearly and coherently and how accurately you convey information about what you heard.

You may take notes while you read and while you listen to the conversations and lectures. You may use your notes to help prepare your response.

Listen carefully to the directions for each question. The directions will not be written on the screen.

For each question, you will be given a short time to prepare your response (15 to 30 seconds, depending on the question). A clock will show how much preparation time is remaining. When the preparation time is up, you will be told to begin your response. A clock will show how much response time is remaining. A message will appear on the screen when the response time has ended.

AT07-01

Some people prefer to buy precooked foods while others prefer to purchase ingredients and then cook by themselves. Which way do you prefer and why? Use details and examples to explain your answer.

PREPARATION TIME
00:00:15

RESPONSE TIME
00:00:45

AT07-02

Martin Hall to Be Renovated

Martin Hall, the home of the History Department, will undergo renovations during summer vacation. The renovations are scheduled to begin on May 20 and are expected to end on August 10. During that time, the building will be closed to all students, faculty, and staff members. All of the classrooms in Martin Hall are being improved. A new reading room is also going to be constructed on the third floor. This room will be for the exclusive usage of History Department faculty, staff, and students.

The woman expresses her opinion about the announcement by the History Department. Explain her opinion and the reasons she gives for holding that opinion.

PREPARATION TIME
00:00:30

RESPONSE TIME
00:00:60

AT07-03

Animal Energy Conservation

All animals possess a finite amount of energy. They must expend it as efficiently as possible to have enough for the tasks they must do each day. For instance, if an animal uses too much energy while hunting, it may be too exhausted to defend itself or to run away if it is attacked. Thus animals must optimize both their energy production and output. The ideal way of doing this is to acquire a food source that can provide a great amount of energy while requiring a small amount of energy to find and obtain.

The professor talks about the cheetah and the orangutan. Explain how their actions are related to animal energy conservation.

PREPARATION TIME
00:00:30

RESPONSE TIME
00:00:60

AT07-04

Using points and examples from the talk, explain the advantages of networking.

PREPARATION TIME
00:00:20

RESPONSE TIME
00:00:60

Actual Test

08

Speaking Section Directions

 Make sure your headset is on.

This section measures your ability to speak about a variety of topics. You will answer four questions by speaking into the microphone. Answer as completely as possible.

In the first question, you will speak about a familiar topic. Your response will be scored on your ability to speak clearly and coherently.

In the next two questions, you will first read a short reading passage. This passage will go away, and you will then listen to a talk on the same topic. You will be asked about the information you have read and heard. You will need to combine information from the reading passage and the talk to provide a complete answer. Your response will be scored on your ability to speak clearly and coherently and how accurately you convey information about what you read and heard.

In the last question, you will listen to part of a lecture. You will be asked about what you have heard. Your response will be scored on your ability to speak clearly and coherently and how accurately you convey information about what you heard.

You may take notes while you read and while you listen to the conversations and lectures. You may use your notes to help prepare your response.

Listen carefully to the directions for each question. The directions will not be written on the screen.

For each question, you will be given a short time to prepare your response (15 to 30 seconds, depending on the question). A clock will show how much preparation time is remaining. When the preparation time is up, you will be told to begin your response. A clock will show how much response time is remaining. A message will appear on the screen when the response time has ended.

AT08-01

Do you agree or disagree with the following statement?

Parents are children's best teachers.

Use details and examples to explain your answer.

PREPARATION TIME
00:00:15

RESPONSE TIME
00:00:45

🎧 AT08-02

City University to Close Archaeology Department

At the conclusion of this semester, the Archaeology Department at City University is going to close. In recent years, enrollment in archaeology classes has steadily decreased. This semester, there are only a total of 109 students enrolled in 12 archaeology classes. As the university needs to improve its financial situation, it has no choice but to close the department. All 6 full-time professors and 2 part-time professors in the department will have their positions terminated and will be free to seek employment elsewhere as of January 1.

The man expresses his opinion about the announcement by the school administration. Explain his opinion and the reasons he gives for holding that opinion.

PREPARATION TIME
00:00:30

RESPONSE TIME
00:00:60

🎧 AT08-03

Boredom

Boredom is the feeling people get when whatever activity they are doing is neither exciting nor interesting. It frequently happens to individuals who repeat the same activities day after day. For instance, people whose daily routines and free-time activities have virtually no variation are prone to suffer from chronic boredom. The same is true for those individuals who always engage in the same activities while they are at their homes. Some of the effects of chronic boredom are depression, loneliness, and sadness. In extreme cases, it can cause people to contemplate suicide.

The professor talks about two of his friends. Explain how their actions are related to boredom.

PREPARATION TIME
00:00:30

RESPONSE TIME
00:00:60

🎧 AT08-04

Using points and examples from the talk, explain two ways in which animals employ mimicry.

PREPARATION TIME
00:00:20

RESPONSE TIME
00:00:60

Actual Test

09

CONTINUE

Speaking Section Directions

 Make sure your headset is on.

This section measures your ability to speak about a variety of topics. You will answer four questions by speaking into the microphone. Answer as completely as possible.

In the first question, you will speak about a familiar topic. Your response will be scored on your ability to speak clearly and coherently.

In the next two questions, you will first read a short reading passage. This passage will go away, and you will then listen to a talk on the same topic. You will be asked about the information you have read and heard. You will need to combine information from the reading passage and the talk to provide a complete answer. Your response will be scored on your ability to speak clearly and coherently and how accurately you convey information about what you read and heard.

In the last question, you will listen to part of a lecture. You will be asked about what you have heard. Your response will be scored on your ability to speak clearly and coherently and how accurately you convey information about what you heard.

You may take notes while you read and while you listen to the conversations and lectures. You may use your notes to help prepare your response.

Listen carefully to the directions for each question. The directions will not be written on the screen.

For each question, you will be given a short time to prepare your response (15 to 30 seconds, depending on the question). A clock will show how much preparation time is remaining. When the preparation time is up, you will be told to begin your response. A clock will show how much response time is remaining. A message will appear on the screen when the response time has ended.

AT09-01

Which would you prefer, to be better at sports than most other people or to excel at creating art? Use details and examples to explain your answer.

PREPARATION TIME
00:00:15

RESPONSE TIME
00:00:45

AT09-02

International Business Internship Program to Begin

The Economics Department is pleased to announce the start of the International Business Internship Program. Every summer, ten of the top sophomore and junior Economics majors at the school will be awarded internships at businesses in Europe, Asia, Australia, and South America. These internships will be unpaid, but the students' airfare and housing will be covered by the university. Students will also receive a small stipend to pay the cost of food while they are abroad. To find out how to apply, visit the Economics Department office in room 104 in Richardson Hall.

The woman expresses her opinion about the announcement by the Economics Department. Explain her opinion and the reasons she gives for holding that opinion.

PREPARATION TIME
00:00:30

RESPONSE TIME
00:00:60

🎧 AT09-03

Parasitic Behavior Alteration

Parasites are organisms which attach themselves to and live off a second organism, called a host. Parasitic behavior is always harmful to the host. In some cases, the parasite can force the host to act in a manner that is atypical. The reason this unusual behavior takes place is not yet clear to scientists. But some speculate that the parasite induces the host to behave in a manner that will benefit the parasite. In some cases, the behavioral change leads directly to the death of the host.

The professor talks about spooked spiders and rats. Explain how their actions are related to parasitic behavior alteration.

PREPARATION TIME
00:00:30

RESPONSE TIME
00:00:60

🎧 AT09-04

Using points and examples from the talk, explain how some businesses are trying to become more ecofriendly.

PREPARATION TIME
00:00:20

RESPONSE TIME
00:00:60

Actual Test

10

Speaking Section Directions

 Make sure your headset is on.

This section measures your ability to speak about a variety of topics. You will answer four questions by speaking into the microphone. Answer as completely as possible.

In the first question, you will speak about a familiar topic. Your response will be scored on your ability to speak clearly and coherently.

In the next two questions, you will first read a short reading passage. This passage will go away, and you will then listen to a talk on the same topic. You will be asked about the information you have read and heard. You will need to combine information from the reading passage and the talk to provide a complete answer. Your response will be scored on your ability to speak clearly and coherently and how accurately you convey information about what you read and heard.

In the last question, you will listen to part of a lecture. You will be asked about what you have heard. Your response will be scored on your ability to speak clearly and coherently and how accurately you convey information about what you heard.

You may take notes while you read and while you listen to the conversations and lectures. You may use your notes to help prepare your response.

Listen carefully to the directions for each question. The directions will not be written on the screen.

For each question, you will be given a short time to prepare your response (15 to 30 seconds, depending on the question). A clock will show how much preparation time is remaining. When the preparation time is up, you will be told to begin your response. A clock will show how much response time is remaining. A message will appear on the screen when the response time has ended.

AT10-01

Do you agree or disagree with the following statement?

Students learn more when they participate in class discussions.

Use details and examples to explain your answer.

PREPARATION TIME
00:00:15

RESPONSE TIME
00:00:45

AT10-02

Morrison Hall to Have Kitchens Installed

This summer, Morrison Hall, the largest dormitory on campus, is going to be closed as it undergoes a significant change. The student lounges, which are located on each floor of the ten-floor building, are going to be converted into kitchens. This will enable students to be able to cook for themselves near their rooms. Every kitchen will be equipped with a stove with four burners, a gas oven, a microwave oven, a refrigerator/freezer, and a variety of pots, pans, dishes, and utensils. The funding for this project is being provided by a donation by the Gibson Foundation.

The woman expresses her opinion about the announcement by the student housing office. Explain her opinion and the reasons she gives for holding that opinion.

PREPARATION TIME
00:00:30

RESPONSE TIME
00:00:60

🎧 AT10-03

Product Demonstrations

Businesses continually look for new ways to sell their products to customers. In modern times, some potential customers can be dismayed by products that appear to be complex, difficult to operate, or hard to understand. To overcome these problems and to convince shoppers to buy their goods, many businesses conduct product demonstrations. These involve a person— or people—demonstrating how easy it is to use various products. Product demonstrations can be performed in person at stores, on the street, and on television commercials. The hope is that these demonstrations will attract new customers for the products being pitched.

The professor talks about an incident involving his family. Explain how it is related to product demonstrations.

PREPARATION TIME
00:00:30

RESPONSE TIME
00:00:60

AT10-04

Using points and examples from the talk, explain two ways that humans help animals as they migrate.

PREPARATION TIME
00:00:20

RESPONSE TIME
00:00:60

Actual Test

11

Speaking Section Directions

 Make sure your headset is on.

This section measures your ability to speak about a variety of topics. You will answer four questions by speaking into the microphone. Answer as completely as possible.

In the first question, you will speak about a familiar topic. Your response will be scored on your ability to speak clearly and coherently.

In the next two questions, you will first read a short reading passage. This passage will go away, and you will then listen to a talk on the same topic. You will be asked about the information you have read and heard. You will need to combine information from the reading passage and the talk to provide a complete answer. Your response will be scored on your ability to speak clearly and coherently and how accurately you convey information about what you read and heard.

In the last question, you will listen to part of a lecture. You will be asked about what you have heard. Your response will be scored on your ability to speak clearly and coherently and how accurately you convey information about what you heard.

You may take notes while you read and while you listen to the conversations and lectures. You may use your notes to help prepare your response.

Listen carefully to the directions for each question. The directions will not be written on the screen.

For each question, you will be given a short time to prepare your response (15 to 30 seconds, depending on the question). A clock will show how much preparation time is remaining. When the preparation time is up, you will be told to begin your response. A clock will show how much response time is remaining. A message will appear on the screen when the response time has ended.

AT11-01

Answer one of the following questions.

1 Some people prefer to socialize with their friends at their homes. Others like to socialize with their friends at other places. Talk about the advantages and disadvantages of socializing with friends at home. Use details and examples to explain your answer.

2 Some people prefer to socialize with their friends at their homes. Others like to socialize with their friends at other places. Talk about the advantages and disadvantages of socializing with friends at other places. Use details and examples to explain your answer.

PREPARATION TIME
00:00:15

RESPONSE TIME
00:00:45

🎧 AT11-02

School to Open Off-Campus Living Office

As a result of numerous requests, the school will open an off-campus living office in December of this year. The office will be located in room 214 in Packard Hall. There will be two full-time staff members and three part-time employees. The workers in the office will provide advice for students who wish to live off campus. This advice will include helping students find sufficient off-campus housing and informing them about the average rents for places in the area. Interested students may call the student housing office at 954-1912 for more information.

The man expresses his opinion about the announcement by the school administration. Explain his opinion and the reasons he gives for holding that opinion.

PREPARATION TIME
00:00:30

RESPONSE TIME
00:00:60

AT11-03

Global Cooling

The Earth's climate constantly undergoes changes. At times, the global climate can be several degrees hotter than it is at the present. At other times, global cooling may occur. When global cooling happens, the average temperature on the entire planet declines several degrees Celsius. As a result, the polar ice caps expand much farther than normal. Places in temperate zones become colder, glaciers extend to cover large amounts of land, and many species die out because they cannot adapt to the weather. Global cooling can take place gradually or may occur suddenly on account of various natural phenomena.

The professor talks about the Mount Tambora eruption. Explain how it is related to global cooling.

PREPARATION TIME
00:00:30

RESPONSE TIME
00:00:60

AT11-04

Using points and examples from the talk, explain two benefits that are provided by commuter trains.

PREPARATION TIME
00:00:20

RESPONSE TIME
00:00:60

Actual Test

12

Speaking Section Directions

 Make sure your headset is on.

This section measures your ability to speak about a variety of topics. You will answer four questions by speaking into the microphone. Answer as completely as possible.

In the first question, you will speak about a familiar topic. Your response will be scored on your ability to speak clearly and coherently.

In the next two questions, you will first read a short reading passage. This passage will go away, and you will then listen to a talk on the same topic. You will be asked about the information you have read and heard. You will need to combine information from the reading passage and the talk to provide a complete answer. Your response will be scored on your ability to speak clearly and coherently and how accurately you convey information about what you read and heard.

In the last question, you will listen to part of a lecture. You will be asked about what you have heard. Your response will be scored on your ability to speak clearly and coherently and how accurately you convey information about what you heard.

You may take notes while you read and while you listen to the conversations and lectures. You may use your notes to help prepare your response.

Listen carefully to the directions for each question. The directions will not be written on the screen.

For each question, you will be given a short time to prepare your response (15 to 30 seconds, depending on the question). A clock will show how much preparation time is remaining. When the preparation time is up, you will be told to begin your response. A clock will show how much response time is remaining. A message will appear on the screen when the response time has ended.

AT12-01

Which is a better way for teachers to evaluate their students?

- **By giving them daily homework assignments that they must submit**

- **By having class discussions and then grading them on their participation**

Use details and examples to explain your answer.

PREPARATION TIME
00:00:15

RESPONSE TIME
00:00:45

AT12-02

All Students Must Do Community Service Every Semester

Effective in the spring semester, all full-time students at City College, including seniors, must do community service. Students must volunteer a minimum of 16 hours per semester. Those students who do not fulfill this requirement will not be permitted to graduate. Students must register the place they will be doing their community service with the dean of students. Each month, they must submit a signed note from a supervisor at the place they are volunteering that states how many hours they have worked. For more information, call 535-1012.

The man expresses his opinion about the announcement by the dean of students. Explain his opinion and the reasons he gives for holding that opinion.

PREPARATION TIME
00:00:30

RESPONSE TIME
00:00:60

AT12-03

The Transfer of Learning

When people learn about something, the knowledge they gain can often assist them in learning about something else. In fact, learning additional information or knowledge—especially that which is more difficult or complicated—becomes easier thanks to the prior knowledge a person has. This is known as the transfer of learning. The transfer of learning is an essential learning method for most individuals. It can be likened to a baby first learning to crawl, then to walk, and finally to run. Each previous step helps lead a person to the next one.

The professor talks about academic and nonacademic learning. Explain how they are related to the transfer of learning.

PREPARATION TIME
00:00:30

RESPONSE TIME
00:00:60

AT12-04

Using points and examples from the talk, explain two reasons that animals form social groups.

PREPARATION TIME
00:00:20

RESPONSE TIME
00:00:60

Actual Test

13

CONTINUE

VOLUME

Speaking Section Directions

 Make sure your headset is on.

This section measures your ability to speak about a variety of topics. You will answer four questions by speaking into the microphone. Answer as completely as possible.

In the first question, you will speak about a familiar topic. Your response will be scored on your ability to speak clearly and coherently.

In the next two questions, you will first read a short reading passage. This passage will go away, and you will then listen to a talk on the same topic. You will be asked about the information you have read and heard. You will need to combine information from the reading passage and the talk to provide a complete answer. Your response will be scored on your ability to speak clearly and coherently and how accurately you convey information about what you read and heard.

In the last question, you will listen to part of a lecture. You will be asked about what you have heard. Your response will be scored on your ability to speak clearly and coherently and how accurately you convey information about what you heard.

You may take notes while you read and while you listen to the conversations and lectures. You may use your notes to help prepare your response.

Listen carefully to the directions for each question. The directions will not be written on the screen.

For each question, you will be given a short time to prepare your response (15 to 30 seconds, depending on the question). A clock will show how much preparation time is remaining. When the preparation time is up, you will be told to begin your response. A clock will show how much response time is remaining. A message will appear on the screen when the response time has ended.

🎧 AT13-01

Which would you prefer, to receive a gift or money for your birthday? Use details and examples to explain your answer.

PREPARATION TIME
00:00:15

RESPONSE TIME
00:00:45

AT13-02

Parking Problems on Campus

I would like to express my unhappiness with the parking situation at the school. There are only a limited number of places on campus where freshmen and sophomores may park their cars. Most of them are located far from the academic buildings on campus. I propose that the school use the area behind Miller Hall as a parking lot. Currently, it is a place with nothing but trees. However, it could easily be converted to a parking lot and would help ease parking problems on campus.

Kevin Sellers

Sophomore

The woman expresses her opinion about the letter to the editor in the school newspaper. Explain her opinion and the reasons she gives for holding that opinion.

PREPARATION TIME
00:00:30

RESPONSE TIME
00:00:60

🎧 AT13-03

The Principle of Allocation

All organisms must efficiently employ their energy to survive. Each organism has a limited amount of energy that it must utilize for reproduction, the acquisition of food, the maintaining of health, the defending of territory, and the protecting of offspring. Natural selection has enabled organisms to evolve in such a way that they effectively manage the amount of energy used for each aspect of their lives. By allocating less energy to less crucial tasks and more energy to more important ones, an organism can ensure both its survival and the propagation of its species.

The professor talks about annual and perennial plants. Explain how they are related to the principle of allocation.

PREPARATION TIME
00:00:30

RESPONSE TIME
00:00:60

AT13-04

Using points and examples from the talk, explain two ways that the domestication of the horse changed society.

PREPARATION TIME

00:00:20

RESPONSE TIME

00:00:60

Actual Test

14

Speaking Section Directions

 Make sure your headset is on.

This section measures your ability to speak about a variety of topics. You will answer four questions by speaking into the microphone. Answer as completely as possible.

In the first question, you will speak about a familiar topic. Your response will be scored on your ability to speak clearly and coherently.

In the next two questions, you will first read a short reading passage. This passage will go away, and you will then listen to a talk on the same topic. You will be asked about the information you have read and heard. You will need to combine information from the reading passage and the talk to provide a complete answer. Your response will be scored on your ability to speak clearly and coherently and how accurately you convey information about what you read and heard.

In the last question, you will listen to part of a lecture. You will be asked about what you have heard. Your response will be scored on your ability to speak clearly and coherently and how accurately you convey information about what you heard.

You may take notes while you read and while you listen to the conversations and lectures. You may use your notes to help prepare your response.

Listen carefully to the directions for each question. The directions will not be written on the screen.

For each question, you will be given a short time to prepare your response (15 to 30 seconds, depending on the question). A clock will show how much preparation time is remaining. When the preparation time is up, you will be told to begin your response. A clock will show how much response time is remaining. A message will appear on the screen when the response time has ended.

AT14-01

Do you agree or disagree with the following statement?

It is necessary for teachers to encourage their students to speak when having class discussions.

Use details and examples to explain your answer.

PREPARATION TIME
00:00:15

RESPONSE TIME
00:00:45

AT14-02

New Energy-Saving Measures to Be Used

Due to the recent increase in the electricity rates, the school will attempt to use as little electricity as possible. Two cost-cutting measures will be implemented immediately. First, until spring arrives, the heat in every academic building on campus will only be turned on from 8 A.M. to noon and from 4 P.M to 8 P.M. Second, starting at 6 P.M., the lights in all classrooms that are not being used are going to be turned off until the next day. Hopefully, both measures will save the school a significant amount of money.

The man expresses his opinion about the announcement by the Building and Grounds Department. Explain his opinion and the reasons he gives for holding that opinion.

PREPARATION TIME
00:00:30

RESPONSE TIME
00:00:60

AT14-03

Social Skills for Children

An essential part of childhood involves learning social skills. Most children learn these skills from their parents as well as their teachers and peers. The key components of childhood social skills are learning to get along with others, to play together, to share, and to lead and follow. Children who grasp these concepts are typically popular with others in their age group whereas those who do not may be ostracized by other children. Those children with poor social skills may lose their friends until they improve their ability to get along well with others.

The professor talks about her past as an elementary school teacher. Explain how it is related to social skills for children.

PREPARATION TIME
00:00:30

RESPONSE TIME
00:00:60

AT14-04

Using points and examples from the talk, explain how some animals have adapted to live in savannahs.

PREPARATION TIME
00:00:20

RESPONSE TIME
00:00:60

Actual Test

15

Speaking Section Directions

 Make sure your headset is on.

This section measures your ability to speak about a variety of topics. You will answer four questions by speaking into the microphone. Answer as completely as possible.

In the first question, you will speak about a familiar topic. Your response will be scored on your ability to speak clearly and coherently.

In the next two questions, you will first read a short reading passage. This passage will go away, and you will then listen to a talk on the same topic. You will be asked about the information you have read and heard. You will need to combine information from the reading passage and the talk to provide a complete answer. Your response will be scored on your ability to speak clearly and coherently and how accurately you convey information about what you read and heard.

In the last question, you will listen to part of a lecture. You will be asked about what you have heard. Your response will be scored on your ability to speak clearly and coherently and how accurately you convey information about what you heard.

You may take notes while you read and while you listen to the conversations and lectures. You may use your notes to help prepare your response.

Listen carefully to the directions for each question. The directions will not be written on the screen.

For each question, you will be given a short time to prepare your response (15 to 30 seconds, depending on the question). A clock will show how much preparation time is remaining. When the preparation time is up, you will be told to begin your response. A clock will show how much response time is remaining. A message will appear on the screen when the response time has ended.

AT15-01

Do you believe it is easier for people to eat healthy food today than it was fifty years ago? Use details and examples to explain your answer.

PREPARATION TIME
00:00:15

RESPONSE TIME
00:00:45

AT15-02

Bicycles Banned on Campus

In the past month, there have been three serious accidents involving bicyclists and motor vehicles. In every case, the bicyclist was at fault for reckless behavior. In addition, this semester, many students have complained about a lack of concern for the safety of pedestrians by bicyclists. As a result, effective Monday, April 10, bicycles are hereby banned from campus. Nobody, including students, faculty, and staff members, may ride a bicycle on campus at any time. Please contact Dean Stan Reynolds if you have any questions concerning this policy.

The man expresses his opinion about the announcement by the dean of students. Explain his opinion and the reasons he gives for holding that opinion.

PREPARATION TIME
00:00:30

RESPONSE TIME
00:00:60

AT15-03

Information Overload

There are some situations in which an individual can receive too much information at once. This information overload can overwhelm the person and result in that individual suffering a great deal of stress. In many instances, when someone suffers from information overload, that individual must choose one of several options in a short period of time. Since the human brain can only process a certain amount of information at once, making the right choice is extremely difficult. This problem has been exacerbated in recent years on account of the vast quantities of information available to people via modern technology.

The professor talks about an incident involving his family. Explain how it is related to information overload.

PREPARATION TIME
00:00:30

RESPONSE TIME
00:00:60

🎧 AT15-04

Using points and examples from the talk, explain two ways that birds build nests to protect themselves and their young from predators.

PREPARATION TIME
00:00:20

RESPONSE TIME
00:00:60

Actual Test

16

Speaking Section Directions

 Make sure your headset is on.

This section measures your ability to speak about a variety of topics. You will answer four questions by speaking into the microphone. Answer as completely as possible.

In the first question, you will speak about a familiar topic. Your response will be scored on your ability to speak clearly and coherently.

In the next two questions, you will first read a short reading passage. This passage will go away, and you will then listen to a talk on the same topic. You will be asked about the information you have read and heard. You will need to combine information from the reading passage and the talk to provide a complete answer. Your response will be scored on your ability to speak clearly and coherently and how accurately you convey information about what you read and heard.

In the last question, you will listen to part of a lecture. You will be asked about what you have heard. Your response will be scored on your ability to speak clearly and coherently and how accurately you convey information about what you heard.

You may take notes while you read and while you listen to the conversations and lectures. You may use your notes to help prepare your response.

Listen carefully to the directions for each question. The directions will not be written on the screen.

For each question, you will be given a short time to prepare your response (15 to 30 seconds, depending on the question). A clock will show how much preparation time is remaining. When the preparation time is up, you will be told to begin your response. A clock will show how much response time is remaining. A message will appear on the screen when the response time has ended.

AT16-01

Imagine that you are taking a trip to a city in a foreign country. Which of the following do you think would be the best way for you to tour the city?

• **You go on a guided tour of the city with a small group of people**

• **You walk around the city by yourself while using a map**

• **You ask a local resident for advice and then go where that person tells you to**

Use details and examples to explain your answer.

PREPARATION TIME
00:00:15

RESPONSE TIME
00:00:45

AT16-02

New Dining Services Policy

Starting next semester, there will be some changes at the cafeterias located on the campus. In addition to the regular food being served, each dining hall will introduce a new corner that will serve ethnic food. The food corners will feature food from Japan, India, Russia, Ethiopia, Brazil, and other countries. As a result of the expanded menu, the prices of meal plans will increase by 15%. This is a reminder that all students living in the dormitories must still purchase at least a basic meal plan. For more information, call 859-1822.

The man expresses his opinion about the announcement by the student dining services office. Explain his opinion and the reasons he gives for holding that opinion.

PREPARATION TIME
00:00:30

RESPONSE TIME
00:00:60

AT16-03

Thermophiles

The majority of animals on the Earth live in moderate temperature conditions. While some
can survive temperatures below zero degrees Celsius or above forty degrees Celsius, most
animals are comfortable living in temperatures between those two numbers. Yet scientists have
discovered some animals which thrive in extremely hot conditions. These animals are known as
thermophiles. Thanks to their high tolerance for heat, thermophiles can survive in some of the
most hostile environments on the planet. Among them are hot deserts, undersea thermal vents,
and even the insides of active volcanoes.

The professor talks about the Saharan silver ant and the desert monitor lizard. Explain how
they are related to thermophiles.

PREPARATION TIME
00:00:30

RESPONSE TIME
00:00:60

AT16-04

Using points and examples from the talk, explain two benefits of companies selling their own products directly to customers.

PREPARATION TIME
00:00:20

RESPONSE TIME
00:00:60

Actual Test

17

Speaking Section Directions

 Make sure your headset is on.

This section measures your ability to speak about a variety of topics. You will answer four questions by speaking into the microphone. Answer as completely as possible.

In the first question, you will speak about a familiar topic. Your response will be scored on your ability to speak clearly and coherently.

In the next two questions, you will first read a short reading passage. This passage will go away, and you will then listen to a talk on the same topic. You will be asked about the information you have read and heard. You will need to combine information from the reading passage and the talk to provide a complete answer. Your response will be scored on your ability to speak clearly and coherently and how accurately you convey information about what you read and heard.

In the last question, you will listen to part of a lecture. You will be asked about what you have heard. Your response will be scored on your ability to speak clearly and coherently and how accurately you convey information about what you heard.

You may take notes while you read and while you listen to the conversations and lectures. You may use your notes to help prepare your response.

Listen carefully to the directions for each question. The directions will not be written on the screen.

For each question, you will be given a short time to prepare your response (15 to 30 seconds, depending on the question). A clock will show how much preparation time is remaining. When the preparation time is up, you will be told to begin your response. A clock will show how much response time is remaining. A message will appear on the screen when the response time has ended.

AT17-01

Which of the following places would you prefer to live in?

- An apartment which is located in the middle of downtown but is very small
- A house in the suburbs which is located far from a big city but has plenty of space

Use details and examples to explain your answer.

PREPARATION TIME
00:00:15

RESPONSE TIME
00:00:45

AT17-02

Train Station to Open on Campus

In a joint project involving the school and the city government, construction on a new train station to open in the southern part of the campus and a railway line is going to begin this Friday. The station, to be located behind Benedict Hall, will be connected to the commuter line going to Freemont Station. Construction on the station and the railway line is anticipated to take up to eleven months to complete. Once the line is operational, students coming from downtown will receive fast, cheap service to the campus.

The woman expresses her opinion about the announcement by the university development office. Explain her opinion and the reasons she gives for holding that opinion.

PREPARATION TIME
00:00:30

RESPONSE TIME
00:00:60

AT17-03

The Holiday Paradox

Most people create only six to nine new memories every two weeks because most of their activities are routine, so they do little out of the ordinary. This can cause time to appear to move quickly. When people travel, they tend to have fun and do new activities. At first, time appears to move quickly because they are enjoying themselves so much. But at the end of their holiday, they have created so many new memories that their time on vacation seems to have been much longer than it was in reality. This is known as the holiday paradox.

The professor talks about her summer trip. Explain how it is related to the holiday paradox.

PREPARATION TIME
00:00:30

RESPONSE TIME
00:00:60

AT17-04

Using points and examples from the talk, explain two disadvantages of licensing to foreign companies.

PREPARATION TIME
00:00:20

RESPONSE TIME
00:00:60

Actual Test

18

Speaking Section Directions

 Make sure your headset is on.

This section measures your ability to speak about a variety of topics. You will answer four questions by speaking into the microphone. Answer as completely as possible.

In the first question, you will speak about a familiar topic. Your response will be scored on your ability to speak clearly and coherently.

In the next two questions, you will first read a short reading passage. This passage will go away, and you will then listen to a talk on the same topic. You will be asked about the information you have read and heard. You will need to combine information from the reading passage and the talk to provide a complete answer. Your response will be scored on your ability to speak clearly and coherently and how accurately you convey information about what you read and heard.

In the last question, you will listen to part of a lecture. You will be asked about what you have heard. Your response will be scored on your ability to speak clearly and coherently and how accurately you convey information about what you heard.

You may take notes while you read and while you listen to the conversations and lectures. You may use your notes to help prepare your response.

Listen carefully to the directions for each question. The directions will not be written on the screen.

For each question, you will be given a short time to prepare your response (15 to 30 seconds, depending on the question). A clock will show how much preparation time is remaining. When the preparation time is up, you will be told to begin your response. A clock will show how much response time is remaining. A message will appear on the screen when the response time has ended.

Answer one of the following questions.

1   Some students prefer to purchase new textbooks each semester while others prefer to
    buy used textbooks. Talk about the advantages and disadvantages of new textbooks.
    Use details and examples to explain your answer.

2   Some students prefer to purchase new textbooks each semester while others prefer to
    buy used textbooks. Talk about the advantages and disadvantages of used textbooks.
    Use details and examples in your answer.

PREPARATION TIME
00:00:15

RESPONSE TIME
00:00:45

AT18-02

Unfair Parking Pass Price Increase

It has come to my attention that the school administration is once again increasing the price of a parking pass for students. I'm completing my junior year here at school, and this will be the third consecutive year that the price of a parking pass has gone up. This is extremely unfair to the members of the student body. There is no public transportation near the school, so those of us who live off campus have no choice but to drive here. The school should reconsider its decision at once.

Regards,
Stephanie Jackson
Junior

The woman expresses her opinion about the letter to the editor in the school newspaper. Explain her opinion and the reasons she gives for holding that opinion.

PREPARATION TIME
00:00:30

RESPONSE TIME
00:00:60

AT18-03

Value Analysis

When a company is designing a new product, it often searches for ways to reduce costs while maintaining the overall effectiveness and efficiency of the item. The company basically determines what the functions of the product should be. Then, it searches for the most inexpensive ways to provide those functions while still maintaining quality and customer satisfaction. If the company is successful at this application of value analysis, it will be able to manufacture a product that provides it with the highest possible profit margin.

The professor talks about his camera. Explain how it is related to value analysis.

PREPARATION TIME
00:00:30

RESPONSE TIME
00:00:60

🎧 AT18-04

Using points and examples from the talk, explain how human actions have affected the sizes of whitetail deer and rats.

PREPARATION TIME
00:00:20

RESPONSE TIME
00:00:60

Actual Test

19

Speaking Section Directions

 Make sure your headset is on.

This section measures your ability to speak about a variety of topics. You will answer four questions by speaking into the microphone. Answer as completely as possible.

In the first question, you will speak about a familiar topic. Your response will be scored on your ability to speak clearly and coherently.

In the next two questions, you will first read a short reading passage. This passage will go away, and you will then listen to a talk on the same topic. You will be asked about the information you have read and heard. You will need to combine information from the reading passage and the talk to provide a complete answer. Your response will be scored on your ability to speak clearly and coherently and how accurately you convey information about what you read and heard.

In the last question, you will listen to part of a lecture. You will be asked about what you have heard. Your response will be scored on your ability to speak clearly and coherently and how accurately you convey information about what you heard.

You may take notes while you read and while you listen to the conversations and lectures. You may use your notes to help prepare your response.

Listen carefully to the directions for each question. The directions will not be written on the screen.

For each question, you will be given a short time to prepare your response (15 to 30 seconds, depending on the question). A clock will show how much preparation time is remaining. When the preparation time is up, you will be told to begin your response. A clock will show how much response time is remaining. A message will appear on the screen when the response time has ended.

AT19-01

You have the opportunity to join a club that meets on the weekend. Which of the following would you prefer to join?

- A reading club that requires members to read one book each week
- A hiking club that goes on long walks in the local area
- A movie club that meets to watch a movie in the evening

Use details and examples to explain your answer.

PREPARATION TIME
00:00:15

RESPONSE TIME
00:00:45

🎧 AT19-02

Online Used Book Market to Open

In response to numerous requests, an online market for used books will be opened and operated by the school starting this May. All full-time and part-time students will be eligible to sell and to purchase books from one another by using the online bookstore. To make a transaction, students must enter their student ID number. Students will be responsible for determining the quality of the book they are getting and the price they will pay for it. All purchases will be nonrefundable. For more information, visit www.centraluniversity.edu/usedbookmarket.

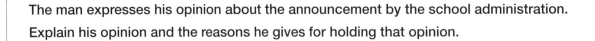

The man expresses his opinion about the announcement by the school administration. Explain his opinion and the reasons he gives for holding that opinion.

PREPARATION TIME
00:00:30

RESPONSE TIME
00:00:60

🎧 AT19-03

Hurdle Help

In track and field, a hurdle is an obstacle that a runner must leap over—often multiple times—in order to complete a race successfully. Children too face obstacles when they attempt to do various tasks. In many cases, a task may require a child to do several steps in order to finish it. Each step is similar to a hurdle in track and field. When a child requires hurdle help, a teacher or instructor provides assistance to enable the child to complete the task.

The professor talks about her time as a kindergarten teacher. Explain how it is related to hurdle help.

PREPARATION TIME
00:00:30

RESPONSE TIME
00:00:60

AT19-04

Using points and examples from the talk, explain how termites can benefit their local ecosystems.

PREPARATION TIME
00:00:20

RESPONSE TIME
00:00:60

Actual Test

20

Speaking Section Directions

 Make sure your headset is on.

This section measures your ability to speak about a variety of topics. You will answer four questions by speaking into the microphone. Answer as completely as possible.

In the first question, you will speak about a familiar topic. Your response will be scored on your ability to speak clearly and coherently.

In the next two questions, you will first read a short reading passage. This passage will go away, and you will then listen to a talk on the same topic. You will be asked about the information you have read and heard. You will need to combine information from the reading passage and the talk to provide a complete answer. Your response will be scored on your ability to speak clearly and coherently and how accurately you convey information about what you read and heard.

In the last question, you will listen to part of a lecture. You will be asked about what you have heard. Your response will be scored on your ability to speak clearly and coherently and how accurately you convey information about what you heard.

You may take notes while you read and while you listen to the conversations and lectures. You may use your notes to help prepare your response.

Listen carefully to the directions for each question. The directions will not be written on the screen.

For each question, you will be given a short time to prepare your response (15 to 30 seconds, depending on the question). A clock will show how much preparation time is remaining. When the preparation time is up, you will be told to begin your response. A clock will show how much response time is remaining. A message will appear on the screen when the response time has ended.

Which of the following assignments would you prefer to complete for a class at school?

• **A group project that requires you to work with others for a month**

• **An individual project that requires you to write a twenty-page paper**

Use details and examples to explain your answer.

PREPARATION TIME
00:00:15

RESPONSE TIME
00:00:45

🎧 AT20-02

Lake Desmond Work Update

The buildings and grounds division has received all of the tables and chairs that it ordered for the Lake Desmond project. This coming weekend, the tables and chairs will be set up in four different areas around the lake. These are to be used exclusively by students, faculty, and members of the administration. Their purpose is to allow people to study and do research outdoors and also to socialize with others. The tables and chairs cannot be reserved and will be available on a first-come, first-served basis.

The man expresses his opinion about the announcement by the buildings and grounds division. Explain his opinion and the reasons he gives for holding that opinion.

PREPARATION TIME
00:00:30

RESPONSE TIME
00:00:60

AT20-03

Pseudoscience

Some people are practitioners of fake science. Science refers to the field of knowledge that can be tested and be proven to be true or false. Pseudoscience, however, uses fake, faulty, or nonexistent evidence. It typically makes claims that cannot be falsified, so it is impossible to test the statements put forth by their adherents. Astrology, which relies upon the locations of celestial objects to make predictions about the future, is an example of pseudoscience. Most types of pseudoscience rely upon stories and claims by people to support themselves.

The professor talks about a role-playing game. Explain how it is related to pseudoscience.

PREPARATION TIME
00:00:30

RESPONSE TIME
00:00:60

AT20-04

Using points and examples from the talk, explain how seed dormancy can benefit plants.

PREPARATION TIME
00:00:20

RESPONSE TIME
00:00:60

Memo

AUTHORS

Michael A. Putlack
- MA in History, Tufts University, Medford, MA, USA
- Expert test developer of TOEFL, TOEIC, and TEPS
- Main author of the Darakwon *How to Master Skills for the TOEFL® iBT* series and *TOEFL® MAP* series

Stephen Poirier
- Candidate for PhD in History, University of Western Ontario, Canada
- Certificate of Professional Technical Writing, Carleton University, Canada
- Co-author of the Darakwon *How to Master Skills for the TOEFL® iBT* series and *TOEFL® MAP* series

Tony Covello
- BA in Political Science, Beloit College, Beloit, WI, USA
- MA in TEFL, International Graduate School of English, Seoul, Korea
- Term instructor at George Mason University Korea, Songdo, Incheon, Korea

Decoding the TOEFL® iBT
Actual Test SPEAKING 1 NEW TOEFL® EDITION

Publisher Chung Kyudo
Editors Kim Minju
Authors Michael A. Putlack, Stephen Poirier, Tony Covello
Proofreader Michael A. Putlack
Designers Koo Soojung, Park Sunyoung

First published in February 2020
By Darakwon, Inc.
Darakwon Bldg., 211, Munbal-ro, Paju-si, Gyeonggi-do 10881
Republic of Korea
Tel: 82-2-736-2031 (Ext. 250)
Fax: 82-2-732-2037

Price ₩16,000
ISBN 978-89-277-0865-0 14740
        978-89-277-0862-9 14740 (set)

www.darakwon.co.kr

Components Test Book / Answer Book
8 7 6 5 4 3 2   21 22 23 24 25

Decoding the TOEFL® iBT

Scripts & Sample Answers

Actual Test

SPEAKING 1

Decoding the **TOEFL**® **iBT**

Actual Test

SPEAKING 1 Scripts & Sample Answers

Actual Test 01

Question 1 p. 9

p. 9

Sample Answer 1

Build a Library

1 use $ to benefit all students
- not all students play sports
- but all students study → library = place to study

2 can do various activities
- read books there
- meet partners for group projects

Sample Response

In my opinion, it would be better for the school to use the donation to build a library rather than to construct a gym. For one thing, the money should be used for something which can benefit all of the students at the school. Not every student plays sports, but everyone at a school studies. By making a library, the school can provide all of its students with a place to study. In addition, libraries are frequently places where students go to do various activities. As for me, I often read books in my school library. And when I have group projects, I usually meet my partners there to do our work. If the school built a library, its students could do the same activities.

Sample Answer 2

Construct a Gym

1 schools train minds and bodies
- my school = gym class 2x/week
- if had gym, could have P.E. more often → fewer students overweight + out of shape

2 sports = fun
- look forward to sports → positive outlook on school
- friend plays sports at school → loves school

Sample Response

If it were my school, I would hope it would construct a gym instead of building a library. For starters, numerous schools ignore the fact that they should be training students' minds and bodies. At my school, we only have gym class twice a week. If we had a gym, we would have P.E. more often. That would help students improve their bodies, so fewer students would be overweight and out of shape. Additionally, playing sports is fun. If students look forward to visiting the gym, they will have a more positive outlook on school as a whole. My friend at another school regularly plays sports at his school's gym, and he loves his school. I wish the same

Question 2 p. 10

p. 10

Listening Script

Now listen to two students discussing the announcement.

M Student: Julie, you're a pre-med student. Are you as unhappy about the decision to make all pre-med students do that internship as most of the other students are?

W Student: On the contrary, I think it's a great decision.

M: Why's that?

W: First of all, doing the internship will be a great way to obtain practical knowledge in the study of medicine. I mean, um, we'll get the opportunity to work side by side with doctors and nurses. That'll be incredible. I expect to learn a great deal during my internship.

M: But aren't you upset about having to do it during the summer?

W: Not really. It doesn't bother me. Instead, I think it will be one of the most important summers of my life.

M: Really? What makes you say that?

W: Simple. I've got the chance to determine if the medical profession is right for me. This internship could affect the course of, well, of my entire life. I'll find out whether going to medical school is what I should do.

Sample Answer

Reading Note

Pre-med juniors must do 2-month internship
- help them decide to go to med school or not
- will do during summer vacation

Listening Note

Woman → likes decision

1 can get practical knowledge
- work with doctors and nurses

2 will be important summer
- can learn if she should go to med school

Sample Response

According to the announcement by the Biology Department, all pre-med students who are juniors at the university have to do an internship at a local hospital. It's a two-month program that has to be completed during the summer. During her conversation with the man, the woman expresses her support for the new program. She gives two reasons for feeling that way. The first reason is that she'll get a great deal of practical knowledge during the internship. She says that she'll attain that knowledge because she'll be working together with doctors and nurses. The second reason is that the internship will help her determine her future career. When she does the internship, she'll be able to decide if she wants to have a future in medicine or not. She states that it will be a big decision, so she is pleased that she'll get to do the internship.

Question 3

p. 11

Listening Script

Now listen to a lecture on this topic in a psychology class.

W Professor: It's never easy to get people to stop doing certain activities. When you tell them not to do something, they typically do the very activity you banned. Let me tell you about how my own children engaged in reactance.

I have a son and a daughter. Three years ago, I bought them a video game machine, but they started playing it too much. Soon, I had to make some rules. They couldn't play video games on schooldays, and they had to do their homework before playing them. Unfortunately, my rules backfired. When I would arrive home from work, they were frequently playing games. They'd also lie to me and say that they'd done their homework when they actually hadn't. Ultimately, I gave the machine away since they wouldn't stop disobeying me.

Soon afterward, my boy started hanging out at the home of one of his friends. He told me they were doing their homework together. But the boy's mother informed me that they were playing video games two or three hours each day. I forbade my son from visiting his friend's home, but he disobeyed my orders. Nearly every week, he would sneak over to his friend's house to play games. Eventually, I had to ground my son for two months to make him stop doing that.

Sample Answer

Reading Note

Reactance

person banned from doing something
- often does that activity
- proves has free will
- can make decisions of his/her own

Listening Note

Tell person not to do something → does that banned activity

1 **bought video game machine for son and daughter**
   - played too much
   - made rules about playing
   - son and daughter broke rules → lied

   - gave game machine away

2 **son started hanging out at friend's house**
   - said was studying
   - was really playing games
   - forbade son from going there → went anyway

Sample Response

The professor tells the students about how her son and daughter reacted after she bought a video game machine for them. They played so many video games that she had to make rules restricting when they could play. However, both children disobeyed their mother, so she decided to give the video game machine to someone else. Then, her son started going to a friend's house a lot. He claimed to be studying, but he was really playing games. She told her son that he couldn't go to that friend's house, but he didn't listen to her and went there anyway. Both incidents involving her son and daughter are examples of reactance. People engage in reactance when they're told they can't do some activity. They engage in the banned activity to prove that they have control over their lives and that others can't tell them what to do.

Question 4

p. 12

Listening Script

Listen to part of a lecture in an environmental science class.

M Professor: Carbon dioxide is a chemical compound formed by the combination of one carbon atom and two atoms of oxygen. It's a naturally occurring greenhouse gas which some people believe may contribute to the warming of the atmosphere. As such, there are numerous attempts to reduce the amount of carbon dioxide that humans release into the atmosphere. Here are a couple of ways people are attempting to do that.

We create the vast majority of our electricity by burning fossil fuels, particularly coal. However, burning coal releases a large amount of carbon dioxide into the air. The best way to reduce the amount of carbon dioxide—as well as various pollutants that the burning of coal releases—entering the atmosphere is to capture or clean it before it ever leaves the factory. Many coal-burning power plants have therefore begun utilizing filtration systems. These devices can trap enormous quantities of carbon dioxide before it's ever emitted. There are several devices. For instance, uh, air filters can capture carbon dioxide. And devices called scrubbers can clean emitted substances so that less carbon dioxide and fewer harmful pollutants are released.

Another method of reducing the amount of carbon dioxide is to plant trees near factories. Why trees . . . ? Well, trees require carbon dioxide to undergo photosynthesis, so, uh, the more trees there are, the less carbon dioxide there is in the atmosphere. Another benefit of this method is that trees produce oxygen in its breathable form, so they simultaneously rid the atmosphere of carbon dioxide and improve the quality of the air. Trees also absorb various particles released by factories, so they further contribute to reducing the amount of air pollution in certain regions.

Sample Answer

Listening Note

Ways to reduce amount of carbon dioxide released

1 **capture or clean it before it leaves factories**
  - use filtration systems
  - can trap carbon dioxide → air filters
  - scrubbers → reduce carbon dioxides and pollutants

2 **plant trees near factories**
  - trees need carbon dioxide for photosynthesis
  - remove it from atmosphere
  - create breathable oxygen

Sample Response

The professor lectures on how people are trying to reduce the amount of carbon dioxide that's released into the atmosphere. Both concern carbon dioxide that's created by humans. First, the professor points out that power plants which burn coal release lots of carbon dioxide. He notes that many of these power plants have started to use filtration systems. He mentions there are both air filters and scrubbers that capture or clean the carbon dioxide before it's released, so they can prevent large amounts of it from ever entering the atmosphere. Second, the professor says that trees are often planted near factories. Trees cannot undergo photosynthesis without carbon dioxide. So the trees remove carbon dioxide from the air and, in the process, create oxygen that can be breathed by humans and animals.

Actual Test 02

Question 1 p. 15

Sample Answer 1

Individual Sports

1 **test self against others**
  - do taekwondo
  - win thanks to own skill

2 **can improve my confidence**
  - won tournament
  - felt like could do anything

Sample Response

I definitely prefer playing individual sports rather than team sports. The first reason I prefer them is that I like to test myself against others. I do taekwondo, a kind of martial art, and I love testing my skills against those of my opponents. If I win a match, it was thanks to my skill. If I lose, then my opponent was better than me, and I have no one to blame but myself. The second reason I like individual sports is that they help me improve my confidence. Once, I defeated eight different opponents and won a taekwondo tournament. I felt like I could achieve anything after that victory. I had so much confidence thanks to my victory in that tournament.

Sample Answer 2

Team Sports

1 **like playing with others**
  - work together as team to win
  - can contribute to victory

2 **have learned about teamwork**
  - get along w/teammates even if dislike them
  - all team members try to win together

Sample Response

Some people prefer individual sports, but I like team sports more. For one thing, I enjoy playing together with others on a team. I play basketball, soccer, and volleyball whenever I have time. In all three sports, the players must work together as a team to win. I love being one of the people who can contribute to a victory by my team. Additionally, I have learned a lot about teamwork since I started participating in team sports. I have learned to get along with my teammates, even the ones I dislike. I may not be friends with them, but that doesn't matter when we're playing a game. Then, we're team members, so we work together to try to win.

Question 2 p. 16

Listening Script

Now listen to two students discussing the article.

W Student: Cliff, good luck in tomorrow's elections. I hope you get elected to the student council.

M Student: Thanks a lot, Wendy.

W: By the way, are those changes mentioned in the paper going to affect you in any way?

M: I'm afraid they might. I'm so mad the administration

made these changes the day before the election.

W: How come?

M: First of all, now that the voting booth has been removed from the library, it means that fewer students are going to be able to vote.

W: Why do you think so?

M: Lots of students spend nearly the entire day in the library. They don't have time to go elsewhere to vote, so many of them won't participate in the election at all.

W: Aha . . . That makes sense.

M: And it's not right that voting is going to end early at the cafeteria. Remember, um, the cafeteria is located near the dorms. So students living in them can easily walk over and vote there. But the student center is practically on the other side of campus. Many students won't want to go there to vote at night.

W: I hadn't considered that.

Sample Answer

Reading Note

Voting changes

- no voting in library
- voting in cafeteria ends at 8, not 9

Listening Note

Man → dislikes decision

1 **students study in library**
   - don't have time to go out
   - won't vote

2 **cafeteria near dorms**
   - easy for students to get to
   - won't go to student center → far away

Sample Response

The man tells the woman he's very upset about the changes described in the student newspaper. According to the newspaper, the school administration has decided that there won't be any voting in the library due to noise considerations and that voting in the school cafeteria will finish early. The man disagrees with both decisions. To begin with, he states that many students study at the library and don't have enough time to leave it. Since they can't vote in the library, it's likely that they won't vote in the election. Then, he points out that the cafeteria is located near the dorms, which makes it easy for most students to vote. However, since voting there will end early, they'll have to travel much farther to get to the student center. As a result, most of the students probably won't vote if they can't do it in the cafeteria.

Question 3

Now listen to a lecture on this topic in a zoology class.

M Professor: Standing out in the wild isn't usually effective. That's why so many animals tend to have the same color as the background in which they live. However, there are some animals which are extremely easy to see. In fact, it's almost as if they actually want predators to see them.

One example is the poison dart frog. It's an amphibian native to Central and South America. Look at the picture here . . . As you can see, it comes in a wide variety of colors . . . and skin patterns . . . but notice that all of them are very bright and distinctive, which makes the frog stand out in its rainforest environment. Normally, this would be a disadvantage, but, um, the frog's colorful skin contains a deadly toxin. Any predators that eat it will die. Predators seem to recognize the danger the frog poses, so, when they suddenly encounter it, they move away from it.

A less lethal example of an animal using coloration to its advantage is this creature . . . the skunk. It can spray a highly offensive-smelling substance from glands in its posterior. Notice the skunk's distinct coloration . . . mostly, uh, black fur with a large bright white stripe on its back . . . Any animal that has had the misfortune of being sprayed by a skunk will instantly recognize other skunks in the future . . . and avoid all contact with them.

Sample Answer

Reading Note

Animal Warning Coloration

animals stand out → warning coloration

- brightly colored fur or skin
- often have poison or venom
- other animals avoid

Listening Note

Some animals → easy to see

1 **poison dart frog**
   - bright and distinctive skin colors and patterns
   - skin → deadly toxin
   - if predator eats, will die
   - predators see frog → move away from it

2 **skunk**
   - sprays bad-smelling substance
   - black fur w/bright white stripe
   - animals recognize → avoid contact

Actual Test 02 **5**

The professor's lecture is about two animals, the poison dart frog and the skunk. Concerning the poison dart frog, he points out how brightly colored it is and therefore how easy it is to see the frog. The professor then states that the frog's skin is highly poisonous, so animals that eat it die. Next, the professor shows a picture of a skunk and points out the distinctive white stripe that runs down its back. He says the skunk can spray animals attacking it with a liquid that smells terrible. Both the poison dart frog and skunk employ animal warning coloration. This refers to bright and distinctive coloring on an animal's skin or fur. This typically indicates that the animal is dangerous in some regard, so predators understand they should avoid these animals so nothing bad happens to them.

Question 4

p. 18

Listen to part of a lecture in a geology class.

W Professor: Humans have been building arches ever since the time of ancient Rome. See here . . . and here . . . I often wonder whether the Romans got the idea from nature since there are naturally occurring arches. Anyway, uh, in geology, an arch is any rock formation that has the appearance of, well, an arch. Natural arches usually occur due to the action of erosion. They mostly form along coastlines and in deserts.

Here's a picture of a coastal arch . . . Coastal arches are formed by the force of water. They may be created when a headland is at around a ninety-degree angle to the waves hitting the shore. Now, um, a headland juts out from the main line of cliffs. Over time, the waves beat on the rocks until they wear it away, which forms a cave. When the waves erode entirely through the cave and break out through the other side, a natural arch forms. Sometimes several arches form in a line, um, like this . . . Over time, many arches collapse and leave lines of what appear to be stacked rocks in the water.

The other main type of natural arch is produced by weathering effects, uh, such as blowing sand and the action of frozen water. In deserts, blowing sand acts like a sandblaster, so, over a long period of time, it can erode rocks to form arches. Another way desert arches form is due to water. Water seeps into small cracks in rocks and then freezes when temperatures drop at night. When the water becomes ice, it expands, so it causes some rocks to break off. Over time, that can produce natural arches like this one here . . .

Listening Note

Arches = can occur naturally

1 **coastal arch**
   - formed by water
   - waves erode headland jutting out from cliffs
   - forms an arch

2 **arches in deserts**
   - formed by weathering effects
   - blowing sand → acts like sandblaster
   - frozen water → expands and makes rocks fall off

The professor tells the students there are two major ways that natural arches may form. The first type of arch she mentions is the coastal arch. It forms when there is some land jutting out into the water. The waves constantly hit this land, so, over time, part of the land gets worn away. First, a cave gets formed, but the water eventually breaks through to the other side and creates a natural arch. The second type of arch the professor discusses is found in deserts. She mentions that weathering effects caused by the blowing of sand and the freezing of water can form this kind of arch. Regarding sand, she says that the sand blasts rock away and makes an arch. As for water, it gets into cracks and freezes at night. As ice, water expands, so it breaks off pieces of rock, which allow it to form an arch.

Actual Test 03

Question 1

p. 21

Location

1 **will live at home**
   - is comfortable
   - can study better there

2 **parents aren't in good health**
   - is duty to take care of them
   - can be near if have medical emergency

For me, the location of a university is much more important than the amount of tuition I have to pay. First, I intend to live at home while I'm attending a university. By living at home, I can be in a comfortable environment. I will be able to study better at home since it's very quiet, unlike many university dormitories. Second, my parents are not in good physical health, so I believe it's my duty to stay near home to help take care of them. By attending a school that's close to my home, I will be able to be near my parents in case one of them has a medical emergency and needs to get to a hospital quickly.

Sample Answer 2

Tuition

1 **family isn't wealthy**
   - can't send me to expensive school
   - must attend cheap school

2 **won't have to work much at cheap school**
   - will get part-time job
   - but only want to work a few hours

Sample Response

The cost of tuition at many universities is rising steadily these days, so it's of greater importance to me than the location of the university I attend. My family isn't wealthy, so my parents can't afford to send me to an expensive school. They've already told me that I'm going to have to attend a school where the cost of tuition is lower than average. In addition, if I enroll at a school which has low tuition, I won't have to work very much during the semester. I intend to get a part-time job while I'm studying, but I don't want to work too many hours. Thus if the tuition at my school is low, I'll only have to work a few hours each week to help pay it.

Question 2
p. 22

Listening Script

Now listen to two students discussing the announcement.

W Student: Did you read the announcement about how the school's planning to tell us about events on campus in the future?

M Student: Yes, I did, but, um, I'm not too pleased about it. What's your opinion?

W: Personally, I feel that it's a splendid idea.

M: Are you serious? Why?

W: First of all, in the past, the school has printed that sort of information in the campus newspaper.

M: Yeah, that's precisely the way I like it.

W: But the problem is that the details of an event can change after they get printed. Then, the students who rely on the newspaper will get the wrong information. Emailed updates will contain the most recent and correct news.

M: Hmm . . . I hadn't considered that. You may have a point.

But what about the fact that not everybody checks email daily?

W: Oh, please. It only takes a few seconds to log in to your email to check for messages. Surely everyone on campus can spend that short amount of time once or twice a day. In addition, people can set up email alerts on their cell phones, so, uh, they'll know when the school's email arrives.

M: Yeah, you're right about that.

Sample Answer

Reading Note

School to email students notices daily
- will be on school events
- info won't be printed in school paper

Listening Note

Woman → likes the decision

1 **event details change**
   - papers print wrong info
   - emailed updates → right info

2 **easy to check email**
   - takes a few seconds
   - email alerts on cell phones

Sample Response

The woman tells the man how she feels about the announcement by the school administration. According to the announcement, the school is going to begin sending daily notices of certain events to students' school email addresses. The administration encourages the students to check their email daily to read these notices. The woman believes it's a good idea and gives two reasons for supporting this new policy. First, she mentions that sometimes the school prints information about on-campus events, but then the information changes. As a result, students who rely on that printed information learn the wrong details. She claims that email will have more accurate information. Next, she says that checking email only takes a few seconds. She believes students can check their email once or twice a day to avoid missing any updates.

Question 3
p. 23

Listening Script

Now listen to a lecture on this topic in a biology class.

W Professor: Okay, um, so I've just explained to you what pheromones are. Now, um . . . why don't I provide you with a couple of examples of them? Pheromones are frequently used by insects to serve a number of purposes. Let's see . . .

Ants often utilize pheromones. One is called the trail

pheromone. Ants use it to make a trail, uh, you know, a path, which other ants can follow. Most of the time, this trail leads to a food source. For instance, perhaps an ant finds some food but isn't able to carry it back to the anthill by itself. What the ant then does is use pheromones to create a trail from the source to the anthill. Other ants detect the trail pheromones and immediately march to the food source to retrieve it. If you've ever seen a group of ants walking in a straight line, they're probably following trail pheromones.

Honeybees make use of something called an, uh, an alarm pheromone. This one helps warn other members of its hive that some sort of danger is near. The honeybee has a gland near its stinger that releases alarm pheromones whenever it stings another insect or larger animal. These pheromones alert all of the honeybees in the vicinity that something dangerous is nearby and that they need to defend their hive against it.

Sample Answer

Reading Note

Pheromones = chemical scents

- many purposes
- only understood by same species
- airborne scents or sprayed onto objects

Listening Note

Pheromones = used by many insects

1 **ants → trail pheromones**
   - ant finds food → too much to carry alone
   - use pheromones → makes path
   - other ants follow path → get food

2 **honeybees → alarm pheromones**
   - warns hive danger is near
   - uses stinger → releases pheromones
   - nearby honeybees look for danger → defend hive

Sample Response

The professor lectures about how ants and honeybees utilize pheromones. According to the reading passage, pheromones are chemical signals released by animals such as insects and mammals. These signals can give other members of the same species messages. These messages may concern food, mating, and warnings of danger. The first insect the professor discusses is the ant. The professor remarks that ants can use trail pheromones. When an individual ant finds a food source too big to carry by itself, it uses these pheromones. Other ants detect the pheromones and make a trail from the anthill to the food source. Likewise, honeybees use a type of alarm pheromone. When a honeybee uses its stinger to attack another animal, it releases pheromones, so nearby honeybees know they may need to act to protect their hive.

Question 4 p. 24

Listening Script

Listen to part of a lecture in a marketing class.

M Professor: Advertising is the art of getting people interested in a product or service so that they will then spend money to acquire that particular product or service. In the field of advertising, there are two primary methods of attracting a customer's attention: visual means and verbal means. Let me tell you about each.

Visual means refers to images designed to attract customers by showing them a product or service. Here's an example of one . . . Years ago, I worked on an advertising campaign for a resort in Mexico. We made a TV commercial, which was an expensive but effective way to advertise the place. In the commercial, we showed views of the beautiful beach . . . the gorgeous sunset . . . people having fun at the resort . . . and the interior and exterior of the resort itself. Those images showed people what they'd be getting for their money. So that commercial utilized visual means of advertising.

As for verbal means, it refers to the words used to convince customers to spend their money on goods or services. Let's go back to that commercial I worked on . . . It had a verbal element, too. I happened to write it. As the images played, the narrator said, "Come to the Sunset Resort, where the water is cool and the sunsets are beautiful." Then, the narrator mentioned the price of staying at the resort, which included the room, various activities, and daily lunch and dinner buffets. Everything written and said in that commercial used verbal means of advertising. Thanks to both its visual and verbal elements, the ad was a big success and attracted many new visitors to the resort.

Sample Answer

Listening Note

Advertising = art of getting people interested in product or service

1 **visual means**
   - made TV commercial for resort
   - showed images of the resort

2 **verbal means**
   - words used in ads
   - described resort
   - can be written or spoken

Sample Response

According to the professor, advertisers can utilize both visual means and verbal means to advertise goods or services. To describe both of them, the professor talks about a commercial he worked on in the past. He starts by describing visual means. He says he helped make an advertisement for a resort in Mexico. So the visual means the commercial used were images of the beach, people doing activities at the resort, the sunset, and the resort itself. Next, he states that the commercial also employed verbal means, which are the words either written or spoken in an ad. The professor says that a narrator described the resort and talked about how much visitors would have to pay to stay at it. He notes that by combining both visual and verbal means, the commercial convinced many tourists to visit the resort.

Actual Test 04

Question 1
p. 27

Sample Answer 1

Agree

1 **love modern technology**
   - fascinating technology comes out
   - have to own it

2 **social standing improves**
   - buy new smartphone → friends think I'm cool
   - am up to date on newest tech

Sample Response

I'm the kind of man who loves buying the latest goods instead of waiting for something better to come out later. First of all, I love modern technology, and there's so much fascinating technology coming out all the time. I simply have to own the newest computer, smartphone, or other electronic device as soon as it's available. Just the other day, I bought a brand-new video game console. It was expensive, but I needed to own it. I also like the fact that my social standing improves when I own the latest goods. My friends all think I'm cool when I tell them I bought a smartphone the day it came out. They love the fact that I'm up to date on the latest technology.

Sample Answer 2

Disagree

1 **price = important**
   - new items = expensive
   - wait several months → cheaper prices

2 **brand-new products have problems**
   - wait for engineers to find them
   - fix problems → buy items

Sample Response

I almost never buy anything right when it comes out. Instead, I prefer to wait a while, and then I buy something better. One reason I do this concerns the price. When a new product comes out, it's often quite expensive. However, a few months later, the price tends to decline, and that's when I purchase it. I just got a really good deal on a laptop computer that came out five months ago. Since it's not so popular anymore, the price decreased a great deal. Another reason I wait is that many brand-new products have numerous problems that need to be solved. By waiting, I can make sure the engineers have found everything that's wrong with the items and then fixed those problems.

Question 2
p. 28

Listening Script

Now listen to two students discussing the letter.

M Student: I love reading the letters to the editor that get printed in the school newspaper.

W Student: Why's that? Because the students make some good points?

M: Not at all. I enjoy them because they often make me laugh.

W: Ah, you're referring to the letter that's about selling food in the dorms, aren't you?

M: Totally. That student's idea simply isn't plausible. For instance, there are ten dorms here on campus. It would be, uh, logistically impossible for the school's dining services to set up kiosks in every single one of them.

W: How do you know that?

M: I work part time at dining services. There aren't enough employees there to man kiosks all day long. It would never work.

W: Okay, but don't you agree that students should have access to healthy food?

M: Sure. And they can do that by going to that supermarket about a hundred meters away from campus. There's healthy food available at it. And that supermarket has low prices, so it's not like they'll be paying too much either.

W: Yeah, I suppose you're right.

Reading Note

All dorms → kiosks selling food during finals

- convenient for students → don't have to disrupt studies
- sell healthy food → students avoid junk food

Listening Note

Man → disagrees w/letter

1 too many dorms

- not enough employees for kiosks in all dorms

2 can visit supermarket

- is near campus
- sells healthy food at low prices

Sample Response

The man finds the letter to the editor in the school newspaper to be amusing, and he disagrees with the argument the letter writer makes. In the letter, the student writes that she would like for the university to set up kiosks in each of the school's dormitories. The kiosks would sell food to students so that they don't have to leave their dormitories. She also wants the kiosks to offer healthy foods, which will let students avoid eating junk food. The man dislikes the student's suggestions for two reasons. First, he points out that the school's dining services doesn't have enough manpower to run kiosks in all ten of the school's dormitories. He knows that since he works there. He also mentions that there's a supermarket very close to the campus. He believes that students can take the time to go there to pick up healthy and cheap food.

Question 3   p. 29

Listening Script

Now listen to a lecture on this topic in a physiology class.

W Professor: Most people suffer from stress at some point in their lives. As students, you probably experience stress for school-related issues. Fortunately, there are ways to overcome stress. Here's how one of my students did that a few years ago.

Around eight years ago, one of my student advisees was having trouble adjusting to life as a freshman. This started affecting him in several ways. Let's see . . . He was late for his classes, partied too much, and had trouble sleeping . . . He stopped eating properly and never turned in any of his assignments on time. When he missed two midterm exams, I realized something was seriously wrong.

I called him in to have a meeting with him. I learned he'd

never been away from home for an extended period of time, so, uh, being in an unfamiliar environment was too difficult for him and was stressing him out. Without his normal support group of family and friends, he felt like no one cared for him and that nothing really mattered. To assist him, I encouraged him to join an on-campus support group. The students in it talked freely about their issues and helped one another overcome them. Then, I had him create a schedule for studying, exercising, and sleeping and follow it. After a while, he got rid of his stress and eventually graduated with honors.

Reading Note

Stress → response to stressor

- feel overwhelmed
- many bodily reactions to stressors
- many ways to ease stress

Listening Note

Ways to overcome stress

1 student advisee

- trouble adjusting to school
- had many problems

2 spoke w/student

- unfamiliar environment → was causing stress
- joined on-campus support group
- made schedule
- got rid of stress

Sample Response

The professor discusses one of her old student advisees with her class. She mentions that his freshman year was very difficult. He had all sorts of problems, including missing classes and failing to do his homework. He even skipped a couple of his midterm exams. The professor talked to the student about his life and determined that he was stressed out. He was in a place that he didn't know well and didn't have any friends or family members around. She helped him deal with his stress by having him join a support group and by making him come up with a schedule for all of his daily activities. Thanks to the professor's help, the student got over his stress. According to the reading passage, stress can overwhelm people. That's exactly how the student felt. And people can get rid of their stress by talking about it, eating and sleeping well, and exercising.

Question 4

p. 30

Listening Script

Listen to part of a lecture in a zoology class.

M Professor: Animals have numerous ways in which they can both defend themselves and hunt prey. For instance, um, some have sharp teeth and claws while others have good eyesight or a sense of smell. Still others can run swiftly, which lets them attack or escape more easily. Yet another method is the use of venom, or poison. Interestingly, venom can be used by animals for both offensive and defensive purposes.

Snakes are the best-known animals to make use of venom for the purpose of hunting. Not all snakes are venomous, but those that are can be quite, um, deadly. Venomous snakes include the rattlesnake, cobra, asp, and black mamba. These snakes typically strike quickly and inject venom into their prey by using their fangs. The result depends upon the type of venom the snake has. Let's see . . . Some venom rapidly kills the bitten animal while other venom slowly kills it. In that case, as the animal weakens, the snake follows it, waits for it to die, and then eats it. And yet other venom paralyzes the victim, so the snake typically consumes that prey while it's still alive.

Unlike snakes, many other animals utilize their venom simply to defend themselves. Bees have venom, but they only use their stingers when being attacked by a predator or to defend their hive if it's under attack. Bee stings are rarely fatal to humans, yet they can kill other species of animals. In addition, many species of jellyfish as well as the stonefish are extremely venomous. Despite the potency of their venom, they don't use it to hunt with. Instead, the jellyfish and stonefish only use their venom to defend themselves from predators attacking them.

Sample Answer

Listening Note

Venom → offensive and defensive purposes

1 **snakes = offensive venom**
   - use venom for hunting
   - inject venom w/fangs
   - may rapidly kill, slowly kill, or paralyze animals

2 **other animals = defensive venom**
   - bees → use venom when they or hive is attacked
   - jellyfish and stonefish → powerful venom but use only to defend themselves

Sample Response

The professor tells the class that many animals use venom. He states that they can use their venom either to attack other animals or to defend themselves from predators. First, he mentions that snakes are animals well known for using venom to attack prey with. Snakes such as rattlesnakes and cobras use their venom by biting other animals and injecting poison into their bodies through their fangs. According to the professor, some venom can kill animals quickly, yet other venom slowly kills them. And some venom just paralyzes animals, so the snakes that use it eat their prey while it can't move. Next, the professor mentions some other animals that only utilize their venom to defend themselves. He states that bees have venom which can kill some animals. He also says that some species of jellyfish and the stonefish are highly venomous, but they only use their venom when they are trying to protect themselves.

Actual Test 05

Question 1

p. 33

Sample Answer 1

Advantages

1 **many interests in common**
   - friends do many things together
   - get along well

2 **have fun doing activities together**

Disadvantages

1 **spending time w/same people = boring**
   - afraid friends will make fun of me

2 **get into arguments**
   - fought w/close friend → group of 5 friends didn't speak

Sample Response

There are both advantages and disadvantages to spending time with friends. As for the benefits, friends often have many interests in common. For example, my friends and I love playing sports, watching action movies, and surfing the Internet, so we get along well. Another advantage is that friends have fun doing various activities together. Regarding the disadvantages, sometimes it's hard to speak openly with friends about problems. In my case, I don't talk about some things because I'm afraid my friends might make fun of me. In addition, friends occasionally get into arguments, which causes problems. Just the other day, I had a fight with a close friend of mine, and that resulted in my group of five friends all not speaking to one another for three days.

Advantages

1 get closer to one another
- family does something every weekend → very close

2 get along well
- family never fights or has arguments

Disadvantages

1 spending time w/same people = boring
- friends do same activities w/parents = no fun

2 frequently stay home
- no exciting or interesting activities

Sample Response

I can think of some advantages and disadvantages to spending time with family members. One advantage is that family members can get closer to one another by doing activities together. My family does something together every weekend, and we're really close. A second advantage is that family members often get along well. That's true of my family, so we never get into fights or have arguments with one another. A disadvantage is that it could be boring constantly spending time with the same people. Some of my friends do the same activities with their parents every weekend, and that's no fun for them. Another drawback is that families frequently just stay home, so family members don't have many opportunities to do exciting or interesting activities.

Question 2 p. 34

Listening Script

Now listen to two students discussing the announcement.

M Student: Wow, this is great news. Someone donated money for students to visit museums and other cultural centers in the city.

W Student: I saw that. But I think the donor is wasting his money.

M: Huh? Surely you can't be serious. I mean, uh, I'd love to see the Monet exhibit at the museum, but I can't afford the admission fee.

W: Well, you can get your admission paid by the school, but you won't be able to understand what you're seeing by yourself. I mean, uh, you'd be much better off going there with a professor of art history who can explain the importance of and symbolism in the paintings.

M: Er . . . I just want to see some nice art. That's it.

W: And there's absolutely no need to donate money for something like free admission to museums. The money

should have been donated for other reasons.

M: Such as . . . ?

W: The computer lab at school has seriously outdated computers. That money could be better used to purchase newer, better, and faster ones.

M: I couldn't disagree with you more.

Sample Answer

Reading Note

School received donation
- students visit city cultural spots
- can have admission fees refunded

Listening Note

Woman → disagrees with decision to use $

1 people can't understand exhibits at museums
- need professor to explain

2 should use $ for other reasons
- school has outdated computers
- should buy new ones

Sample Response

The woman tells the man she disagrees with the announcement made by the dean of students. According to the announcement, thanks to a donor, students can now visit cultural sites such as museums and art galleries for free. They need to apply before they go to a place, and then they can get their ticket money refunded by the school. The woman believes the donation is a waste of money and provides the man with two reasons for feeling that way. To begin with, she insists that students will waste their time by visiting art galleries by themselves. She thinks they need an expert to tell them about the art they're viewing. Secondly, she thinks the school should use the money for more important purposes. In her opinion, it would be more ideal for the school to purchase new computers for the computer lab since the ones it has are too old.

Question 3 p. 35

Listening Script

Now listen to a lecture on this topic in a biology class.

M Professor: This animal here on the screen . . . is one of, um, one of the most unusual creatures in the world. It's the lungfish, and it's native to Africa, South America, and Australia. What makes it unusual . . . ? Simple . . . It has gills like a fish and either one or two lungs, um, depending upon the species.

The lungfish evolved to be that way because of its

environment. It lives in regions where arid weather is the norm. When the water dries up, most fish die. But the lungfish doesn't. Here's how it manages to stay alive . . . First, it digs a hole in some mud. Then, it burrows into the mud but leaves a small opening near its mouth. Next, it secretes a gel-like substance that's a kind of mucus. It covers the lungfish's entire body—uh, except for its mouth so that it can breathe air—and keeps the fish cool during the heat of the dry season.

Now, the lungfish enters a state of dormancy. It reduces its metabolism a great deal, so it barely uses any energy. The lungfish then remains in its burrow until the rains return and water is once more present in sufficient amounts. Thanks to its ability to survive in environments where there are both extreme heat and drought, the lungfish prospers while other species perish.

Sample Answer

Reading Note

Dormancy → reduce metabolic activity greatly

- environmental factors cause stress
- reduce activity → save energy
- stay dormant for long periods of time

Listening Note

Lungfish → has gills and lungs

lives in arid environment

- water dries up
- digs hole in mud → burrows into it
- covers body with gel-like substance → stays cool

dormancy

- reduces metabolism → barely uses energy
- stays in burrow until rains return

Sample Response

The professor discusses the lungfish with the class. The lungfish has both gills and lungs, so it can breathe with either of them. According to the professor, the lungfish lives in places that get hot, dry weather. When the dry season begins and the water dries up, the lungfish digs a hole in the mud and buries itself in it. Then, it uses its lungs to breathe air. While it does this, the lungfish becomes dormant. When this happens, the lungfish slows down its metabolism very much, which means that it uses only a small amount of energy. When the rainy season begins, the lungfish can then exit its state of dormancy. Most animals that use dormancy do that because of environmental factors such as hot or cold temperatures or dry weather. By slowing down their metabolism, they consume little energy, which enables them to remain alive despite poor conditions.

Question 4

p. 36

Listening Script

Listen to part of a lecture in a marketing class.

W Professor: Every day, people buy products they need and want. Normally, there are a variety of products to choose from. So, uh, how do people decide what to buy . . . ? Well, that's usually where advertising plays a role. It's a huge industry whose sole purpose is to persuade people to buy certain goods and services. There are many methods of advertising . . . TV and radio commercials, Internet ads, newspaper and magazine ads, flyers, and huge billboards. However, for the most part, advertising is extremely wasteful.

First, let's consider how much paper is used in advertising. Those of you with cars have surely had to remove numerous flyers after they were tucked under your windshield wipers. You've also probably been handed flyers on the street and at subway entrances. What did you do with those flyers . . . ? That's right. You probably threw them away without looking at them, uh, like most people do. And consider all the ads posted on bulletin boards and the posters attached to walls, fences, and other places. All in all, it's a huge waste of paper, and it's responsible for the cutting down of millions of trees a year.

Another advertising problem concerns billboards. First, they're eyesores. You see signs on interstates and highways while driving on them. In cities, billboards seem to be advertising the latest movie or TV show or selling some kind of soft drink or fast food practically, uh, everywhere. Well, in addition to being sources of visual pollution, many billboards are made of wood and plastic products. The electronic ones utilize a great deal of electricity, too. Simply put, these billboards waste energy and natural resources while influencing only a small number of people.

Sample Answer

Listening Note

Advertising = very wasteful

1 **waste of paper**
   - flyers → on cars / given on streets and subway entrances
   - most people throw away

2 **billboards**
   - eyesores → form of visual pollution
   - made of wood and plastic → waste energy and natural resources

During her lecture, the professor tells the students that a great deal of the advertising that's done these days is very wasteful. She provides two examples to defend her argument. First of all, the professor points out the large amount of paper that is wasted to make advertisements. She states that students have most likely been given ads while walking down the street or going to the subway station, but they probably just threw the ads away like most other people do. She comments that there are all kinds of ads placed everywhere, and she claims it requires millions of trees each year to make the paper the ads are printed on. Next, the professor talks about the billboards on the sides of roads and in cities. She says that they not only waste electricity but that they also use important natural resources while having little effect on consumers.

Actual Test 06

Question 1
p. 39

Sample Answer 1

Agree

1 young children = irresponsible
- may lose or break phones
- 6-year-old cousin → lost phone 2 days after getting it

2 cell phones have many functions
- can use Internet
- young children shouldn't use Internet unsupervised

Sample Response

I agree wholeheartedly with the statement. In my opinion, children have absolutely no need to own cell phones. For one thing, most young children are irresponsible while cell phones are expensive. Thus children who own cell phones often lose or break them, which means that the children's parents wasted a considerable amount of money on the phones. My six-year-old cousin got a phone from his parents, and he lost it two days later. They weren't happy about that at all. For another thing, cell phones today have numerous functions, including being able to use the Internet. Young children shouldn't have unsupervised access to the Internet, so it's a bad idea for parents to allow their young children to have cell phones.

Sample Answer 2

Disagree

1 emergency situations
- neighborhood girl got lost
- called for help on cell phone

2 contact family members
- little brother has
- calls parents to get picked up

Sample Response

I disagree with the statement and believe it's all right for young children to own cell phones. The first reason I feel this way is that young children might need to make a phone call in an emergency situation. A couple of weeks ago, a young girl in my neighborhood got lost in the forest in a national park. Fortunately, she had her cell phone with her, so she called for help and was rescued without any problems. The second reason I support letting young children own cell phones is that they may need the phones to contact one of their family members. My little brother owns a cell phone, and he regularly uses it to call my parents to ask them to pick him up after school or sports practice.

Question 2
p. 40

Listening Script

Now listen to two students discussing the letter.

W Student: Mark, you rent bicycles here on campus sometimes, don't you?

M Student: I sure do. Why do you ask?

W: Did you read that letter to the editor in today's paper?

M: Yeah, I saw it.

W: What was your opinion of it?

M: The student didn't really think very hard about the points he made. For instance, um, it sounds great to tell the school to lower the price of the rental fee. However, if the school does that, then students will keep the bikes much longer.

W: So . . . uh, what's wrong with that?

M: The school has a limited number of bikes to rent. There are, um, forty or so, I believe. If students rent them for longer, then many others won't get to use them at all.

W: Aha . . . Well, what about the other point he made?

M: I thought it was sort of silly.

W: Why?

M: We need our ID cards to get into the dorms, the library, and several other buildings on campus. If I leave my ID card at the bicycle rental office, how am I ever going to get into half the buildings here?

Reading Note

Make changes to school's bike rental program

- reduce price → more students can rent bikes
- leave school ID card as deposit instead of $30

Listening Note

Man → disagrees with letter writer

1 **if lower rental fee, students keep bikes longer**
   - only 40 bikes
   - fewer students will rent bikes

2 **need ID card to get into most buildings**
   - if leave ID card as deposit, can't enter many places

Sample Response

The man makes some comments to the woman concerning a letter to the editor both of them read in the school newspaper. The letter writer comments on the bicycle rental program at the school. He wants the school to lower the hourly rate and to let students leave their ID cards in lieu of a cash deposit. The man disagrees with both of the letter writer's points and tells the woman why he feels that way. First, if the school lowers the rental fee, he believes students will keep the bikes for longer periods of time. As a result, many students won't ever be able to rent a bike. In addition, the man points out that the students must have their ID cards to get into numerous buildings on campus, including the dorms and library. If they leave their ID cards as deposits, they won't be able to enter those buildings.

Question 3
p. 41

Listening Script

Now listen to a lecture on this topic in an economics class.

W Professor: Most companies engage in a daily struggle for survival. One problem many of them face is that they don't know their customers. This can be a fatal problem yet can be overcome. Here's an example of what I'm talking about . . .

Recently, a national video and DVD retailer encountered some problems. When high-speed Internet service became prevalent roughly, hmm, a decade or so ago, the company suddenly began losing money. Sales declined dramatically, but the company didn't know why. So it conducted some market research. It surveyed its customers and other people around the country. When the results came in, the executives learned that many people had no desire to drive to a video store to pick up and return movies. They considered doing that a waste of time.

The survey results further indicated that people would

be willing to pay for a secure way to download or stream movies online. After some discussion, the company abruptly changed its business model. It shut down its physical stores and moved its presence, uh, online. Now, it provides movies online in a streaming format. People still pay the company to rent movies from it, but they don't have to leave the comfort of their homes to do so. Thanks to the company's market research, it was not only saved from bankruptcy but is also thriving today.

Sample Answer

Reading Note

Market Research → conducting of surveys

- lets companies know what people want
- can keep current customers and attract new ones

Listening Note

Companies often don't know customers

video and DVD retailer → started losing money

- conducted market research
- customers didn't want to drive to video store

more results

- people will pay $ to download or stream movies online
- company closed stores → moved online
- thriving today

Sample Response

At the start of the professor's lecture, she comments that companies which don't know their customers will experience problems. Then, she discusses the experience of a national video and DVD retailer to give an example of that. She points out that the company began losing money once high-speed Internet became more common. The company decided to conduct some market research to figure out why it was losing money. Market research typically utilizes surveys which can be conducted in a variety of manners. The results of these surveys are used by companies to figure out what their current and potential customers want so that the companies can provide them with it. That's exactly what the company did. Its customers didn't want to travel to video stores, so the company closed its stores and started renting movies to people on the Internet. Thanks to its market research, the company is making money today.

Question 4
p. 42

Listening Script

Listen to part of a lecture in a marine biology class.

M Professor: Fish, especially large ones such as, um, tuna and sharks, can weigh a lot. A great white shark, for instance, can weigh more than two tons. So . . . how do fish float in the water? I mean, uh, why don't they just sink since they're so heavy . . . ? Well, there are a couple of ways they can manage to float.

The first one is to use a swim bladder, which is, hmm . . . it's sort of like the lungs mammals have. Basically, it's a sac which fish can fill with oxygen. Fish acquire oxygen from water that passes over their gills and enters their bodies. Then, much of the oxygen goes into the fish's blood system while some of it ends up in the swim bladder. Whenever the bladder inflates, it provides the fish with extra buoyancy without adding much, um, extra weight. To remain at a certain depth in the water—you know, to float—the fish simply inflates the bladder to a certain point. When the fish subsequently adds more oxygen to the bladder, it rises, and when oxygen is removed from the bladder, it sinks.

Some fish, such as sharks, don't have swim bladders. So what do they do . . . ? They use their horizontal side fins—called pectoral fins—to stay afloat. These fins are shaped like the wings of airplanes, so they can therefore create lift. As water slides over and under them, the shark adjusts the positions of the fins to allow itself to rise, sink, or stay at the same level. The only drawback is that a fish using this method must constantly be swimming, or it will sink to the bottom of the ocean.

Sample Answer

Listening Note

Fish are heavy → don't sink but can float

1 **swim bladder**
   - like lungs of mammals
   - sac that fills w/oxygen
   - can use bladder to float, go higher, and go lower
   - manipulate amount of oxygen in bladder

2 **pectoral fins**
   - fins on the side of fish
   - used by sharks
   - like airplane wings → create lift
   - can rise, sink, or stay at same level
   - fish must constantly be moving

Sample Response

The professor tells the students there are two ways that fish, despite being heavy, can float in the water. The first of these ways is by using a swim bladder. The swim bladder operates like the lungs in mammals do. When the fish wants to float in the water, it fills the bladder with a certain amount of oxygen. In order to go higher in the water, more oxygen can be added to the bladder while oxygen can be removed to allow the fish to descend into the water. If a fish lacks a swim bladder, it uses its pectoral fins instead. These are

fins on the side of the fish's body. Sharks are one type of fish which use their pectoral fins. The pectoral fins act like airplane wings by creating lift for the fish. By remaining in constant motion, a fish can float, swim higher, or swim lower simply by moving its pectoral fins.

Actual Test 07

Question 1   p. 45

Sample Answer 1

Buying Precooked Foods

1 **very busy**
   - go to school and have job
   - no time to cook

2 **precooked food quality is good**
   - just heat in oven or microwave
   - taste better than food I make

Sample Response

I strongly prefer buying precooked foods to purchasing ingredients and cooking meals by myself. First, I am extremely busy. I attend school all day long, and, when I get home, I have homework to do. I also have a part-time job I do on both Saturday and Sunday. I simply don't have time to cook my own meals. So I prefer precooked foods instead. Next, in recent years, the quality of precooked foods has really increased. Some supermarkets sell gourmet prepared meals that only need to be heated in an oven or microwave. Those meals taste better than anything I could ever make and are also incredibly cheap.

Sample Answer 2

Purchasing Ingredients and Cooking by Myself

1 **cooking = relaxing**
   - enjoying making meals
   - made lasagna → had fun

2 **can control what I eat**
   - processed foods = bad for health
   - prefer fresh meats, vegetables, and fruits

Sample Response

Even though I'm really busy, I enjoy purchasing ingredients at the supermarket and cooking my own meals instead of buying precooked foods and heating them in the oven. One of the reasons is that cooking is relaxing for me. I enjoy putting different ingredients together and then making something for an hour or so. Last night, I made lasagna and enjoyed the entire cooking process. A second reason is that I can control what I eat if I prepare my meals by myself. These days, there are all kinds of processed foods, which aren't good for your health. I prefer to eat fresh meats, vegetables, and fruits. So when I cook my own meals, I know I am eating something that tastes good and is also nutritious.

Question 2

p. 46

Listening Script

Now listen to two students discussing the announcement.

W Student: You know, I really wish the school would stop wasting so much money.

M Student: What's going on now?

W: I'm referring to the renovations at Martin Hall. They're a complete waste of money.

M: Are you sure? I have a class in Martin Hall, and the room is, well, terrible. It could use improving.

W: I disagree. I'm a History major, so I take classes in Martin Hall every semester. Sure, um, the rooms aren't in the greatest condition, but they're just lecture halls. It's not like the professors need any kind of special equipment to teach their classes.

M: I suppose.

W: It's true. I don't care about the quality of the rooms. I care about the quality of the lectures.

M: I couldn't agree with you more regarding that.

W: And another thing . . . Have you noticed that tuition is going up again next year?

M: Again?

W: Yes, again. If the school wouldn't do projects like this, it wouldn't need to raise tuition so much. This school is getting too expensive for me to afford.

Sample Answer

Reading Note

Renovations to Martin Hall
- classrooms → improved
- build new reading room

Listening Note

Woman → dislikes renovations

1 classrooms in Martin Hall are okay
 - only need lecture halls
 - don't need special equipment

2 tuition going up
- if no renovations, tuition doesn't go up
- school becoming too expensive

Sample Response

The woman is displeased with the announcement by the History Department. According to it, the school intends to renovate Martin Hall. It's going to make all of the classrooms nicer, and it's also going to build a reading room for the History Department to use. The woman tells the man that she thinks the school is wasting money by doing the renovations. She gives him two reasons for feeling that way. The first one is that she says the rooms in Martin Hall aren't in poor condition. As a History major, she takes classes there every semester. She remarks that the rooms are sufficient since the professors don't need any special equipment while giving their lectures. She also points out that the school is increasing tuition. She believes that if the school would stop doing projects like the renovation of Martin Hall, then tuition wouldn't have to go up so often.

Question 3

p. 47

Listening Script

Now listen to a lecture on this topic in a zoology class.

M Professor: Animals must acquire food by hunting or foraging, or else they'll die. Acquiring food, especially by hunting, can require an enormous expenditure of energy. Over time, however, many animals have evolved to use their energy efficiently.

Let's consider the cheetah . . . It's the world's fastest animal, but it can expend a tremendous amount of energy while running at high speed and pursuing prey. If the cheetah fails quickly to bring down its prey, it will suddenly cease chasing it. Why does it do that . . . ? Well, um, it simply cannot afford to expend too much energy lest it become exhausted to the point that it's defenseless. However, if the cheetah catches its prey, it can replenish the stores of energy which were used in pursuing it.

While the cheetah utilizes tremendous amounts of energy in sudden bursts, the orangutan acts much differently. It hardly even uses one percent of its energy on a daily basis. You see, um, it lives in tropical rainforests and mostly eats fruit, which isn't always available. Thus it has developed a slow metabolism, so it expends energy quite slowly. The orangutan can survive without eating for a long time since it uses very little energy. And, um, when it eats, it consumes fruit that contains high amounts of calories. This fattens it up and leaves it prepared for times when no fruit is available.

Reading Note

Animal Energy Conservation

animals must use energy efficiently

- optimize energy production and output
- acquire food source → provides lots of energy but requires little energy to get

Listening Note

Animals must get food or will die → use energy efficiently

1 **cheetah**
   - will stop chasing prey if can't catch it quickly
   - can't afford to spend too much energy
   - catches prey → replenishes energy used to catch it

2 **orangutan**
   - uses little energy each day
   - slow metabolism
   - eats fruit → can survive long time w/out eating

Sample Response

The professor describes how two animals expend energy in his lecture. In talking about the cheetah, he points out that it can run faster than all other animals. However, if the cheetah fails to catch its prey quickly, it will stop its pursuit. The reason is that the cheetah can't use too much energy or it won't have enough to defend itself. Yet when the cheetah catches an animal, it can restore the energy it lost during the chase. In discussing the orangutan, the professor notes that it barely uses any energy. It simply eats fruit that's high in calories. Since it uses so little energy, it can go long periods of time without eating any fruit at all. Both the cheetah and the orangutan are good examples of animal energy conservation. They both spend as little energy as possible when doing various tasks so that they will have sufficient amounts of energy remaining.

Question 4 p. 48

Listening Script

Listen to part of a lecture in an economics class.

W Professor: One word often heard uttered by businessmen and women is networking. For those of you who don't know, networking is the act of making friends and acquaintances in your field of work or expertise. There are numerous ways to network. Let's see . . . Uh, attending conferences is one way. Joining clubs and associations related to your work is another. And, of course, there are the connections people make at their jobs. You know, uh, customers, people referred to you, and even colleagues. Those people can all become part of your network.

Networking is important because it provides many advantages. Foremost among them is that it can help advance your career. Many of the people you meet in your line of work can make you become better in some way. Certain people can provide advice and assist you in overcoming obstacles. They might also know someone else who can provide assistance if they can't. When I worked in the computer industry, I received constant help from people in my network. Thanks to them, I made it all the way to vice president of my company until I retired to become a professor.

Networking can also improve your image by raising your profile as more people get to know you and learn how good you are at your job. This has several benefits . . . First, it will boost your self-confidence and provide you with a sense of satisfaction. It will additionally result in people coming to you for advice. If you're the go-to person in an office, upper management will notice, which will help you get promoted. And that's exactly what you want when you're employed in the business world.

Listening Note

Networking = act of making friends and acquaintances in work

1 **can advance career**
   - meet people → can make you better
   - provide assistance
   - got help from others in network

2 **improve your image**
   - boost your self-confidence
   - people will come to you for advice
   - bosses notices → get promoted

Sample Response

In her lecture, the professor tells the students about various ways people do networking, and then she discusses two of its advantages. The first benefit she covers is how networking can let people get ahead in their careers. She says that the people an individual becomes acquainted with can help that person in various ways. The people in a person's network can provide good advice and help. They can also introduce others to a person if they are unable to provide assistance themselves. By using personal networks, a person can often get ahead. The second advantage the professor discusses is how networking can improve a person's profile. She points out that it's good to let people know how well you can perform at your job. For example, when others in a person's network go to that person for help, the bosses will notice and be more likely to promote that particular individual.

Question 1   p. 51

Sample Answer 1

Agree

1 parents can set good examples
- can teach children many things
- parents work hard and are polite → taught me to do that

2 parents know children well
- understand how they learn
- taught sisters according to their abilities

Sample Response

I believe that parents are children's best teachers, so I agree with the statement. In most cases, children want to be like their parents. Parents can therefore set good examples for their children through their actions. In that way, they are teaching their children a number of things. My father and mother always work hard and are polite to everyone, so I have learned to act the same way. I couldn't have learned those lessons from anyone else. Parents also know their children better than everyone else, so they understand how to teach their children. My older sister is a textual person whereas my younger sister likes learning from videos. My parents recognized these characteristics and others, so they taught my sisters according to how they best learn.

Sample Answer 2

Disagree

1 children behave poorly & do badly at school
- blame parents for actions
- don't teach children manners and desire to do well at school

2 teachers are better than parents
- have learned how to instruct children
- know how to get them to learn

Sample Response

I thought about agreeing with the statement at first, but now that I think of it, I disagree. I don't believe that parents are children's best teachers. One reason is that I see many children these days who behave poorly and do terribly at school. I blame their parents for their actions. Parents who cannot even teach their children good manners and don't instill in their children a desire to do well at school are clearly awful teachers. In addition, I believe teachers are better at instructing young children than parents are. Most teachers have spent years learning how to instruct children, so they know how to get children to learn. Many parents may want to teach their children well, but they're simply not as good as teachers.

Question 2   p. 52

Listening Script

Now listen to two students discussing the announcement.

W Student: Doug, it doesn't look like you're going to get to take that archaeology course you're interested in next semester. The school is closing the entire department.

M Student: Yeah, I saw the announcement.

W: According to it, enrollment in the department's classes is too low to justify the cost.

M: That makes a lot of sense.

W: Really? I thought you'd be opposed to the decision.

M: On a personal level, it's, uh, disappointing I won't get to take the class. But according to the notice, the department has eight professors. There's no excuse for the school to be paying that many professors if enrollment is so tiny.

W: Yeah, that's how I feel.

M: Furthermore, perhaps another department will be able to utilize the space that the Archaeology Department won't be using.

W: Um . . . what exactly do you mean?

M: My best friend here is an engineering major. He says there isn't enough room for all of their classes since enrollment in the engineering school is increasing. Maybe some engineering classes can be taught in the classrooms the Archaeology Department currently uses. That would give the engineering school some much-needed space.

Sample Answer

Reading Note

Archaeology Department to close

- enrollment → steadily decreasing
- 8 professors but only 109 students in 12 classes

Listening Note

Man → agrees with decision

1 too many teachers and too few students
- school wasting $ on all the professors

2 engineering school needs more space
- enrollment increasing
- can use classrooms that Archaeology Department now uses

The man and the woman discuss a recent announcement by the school administration. It states that the school's Archaeology Department is going to close at the end of the semester. The reasons provided for the closing are that enrollment in the department's classes has steadily decreased and that the school needs to focus on improving its financial condition. The man tells the woman two reasons explaining why he supports the decision. The first point is that he considers the school to be wasting money by employing eight professors since enrollment in the department's classes is so small. The second point the man makes concerns the engineering school. According to his friend, enrollment at the engineering school is increasing, so there isn't enough room for all of its classes. The man thinks the engineering classes could be held in the rooms presently being used by the Archaeology Department.

Question 3

p. 53

Listening Script

Now listen to a lecture on this topic in a psychology class.

M Professor: One of the worst things that can happen to a person who gets into a regular routine is that the individual will suffer from boredom. As you just read in the handout I gave you, a bored person can suffer, um, from a number of unfortunate symptoms. Fortunately, there are ways to change your regular routine and thereby avoid being bored.

One of my friends enjoys exercising. He used to run on his treadmill every day and lift weights three times a week. He did the same thing for a couple of years though, so he started getting, uh, bored. I suggested that he change his routine to make it more interesting. He followed my advice and started walking outdoors instead of using his treadmill. He took up kickboxing and lifted weights less often. Later, he told me that he loved his new routine and wasn't bored anymore.

Another friend did the same thing every day. He got up at the same time . . . ate the same foods . . . went to the same places . . . He became highly depressed by the predictability of his life. Like I did with my other friend, I advised him to stop doing those activities. So he varied when he woke up. He quit having the same foods every day. He visited some new places. These were minor changes, but they had a tremendous effect and ended his boredom.

Sample Answer

Reading Note

Boredom → happens when activity is not exciting or interesting

- do same activities every day
- causes depression, loneliness, and sadness

Listening Note

Bored person → can change routine

1 **friend bored with exercises**
   - suggested changing routine
   - walked instead of using treadmill
   - kickboxing instead of lifting weights
   - love routine → wasn't bored

2 **friend did same things every day**
   - advised to stop
   - woke up at different times
   - ate different foods
   - visited different places
   - ended boredom

During his lecture, the professor tells the class about a couple of his friends that suffered from boredom, and then he explains how they were both able to overcome their feelings of boredom. The first friend liked exercising, but after two years of doing the same exercises, he became bored with them. The professor recommended that he take up other exercises. The man did that, and he found that he enjoyed exercising again and was no longer bored. The second friend did the same daily activities all the time. Since he was bored, the professor gave the man some advice. He changed the way he lived his life and stopped being bored. Both examples show how people can suffer from boredom when they do the same activities again and again. When they suffered from chronic boredom, their lives became affected in a negative manner.

Question 4

p. 54

Listening Script

Listen to part of a lecture in a zoology class.

W Professor: Many animals protect themselves from predators through the usage of mimicry. In case you don't know, there are a variety of ways animals can use mimicry. They can act like other animals. Or they can resemble natural things such as, um, rocks, tree branches, leaves, or even other organisms. Let me give you some examples of two different ways in which animals use mimicry to protect themselves.

Many animals employ mimicry in order to camouflage themselves so that they can hide from the predators that are hunting them. For instance . . . the walking stick is an insect that looks, well, like a stick. This lets it hide in plain sight as animals that might eat it simply do not notice the insect even if they're on the same tree branch as it. Lots of butterflies and moths use mimicry, too. Their wings may resemble tree leaves in shape and color, which enables them to blend into the forest background. Additionally, the stonefish resembles a lumpy rock, so it can lie unseen on the seafloor.

There's another interesting manner in which animals utilize mimicry. In this case, they mimic more dangerous animals by resembling them in appearance. This causes other animals to leave them alone. The robber fly imitates the more dangerous bumblebee both in sound and appearance. The hawk moth caterpillar can shape its head to give it the appearance of a snake. And here's one of my favorites: the scarlet king snake. It lives in the southeastern part of the United States. It has bands of color that make it appear to be the highly venomous coral snake. But the scarlet king snake actually has no venom at all.

Sample Answer

Listening Note

Mimicry = protects animals

1 used as camouflage → hide from predators
   - walking stick → looks like stick
   - butterflies and moths → wings looks like leaves
   - stonefish → looks like rock

2 mimic dangerous animals in appearance
   - robber fly → imitates bumblebee
   - hawk moth caterpillar → head shaped like snake's
   - scarlet king snake → looks like coral snake

Sample Response

During her lecture, the professor tells the students about how some animals use mimicry. This refers to ways in which certain animals act like or resemble other animals or objects. First, she talks about how some animals employ mimicry to camouflage themselves so that predators can't find them. She points out that the walking stick looks like a tree branch, so many animals don't notice that insect. She also mentions that a lot of butterflies and moths resemble tree leaves while the stonefish looks like a rock. The second mimicry method that she covers concerns how certain animals may resemble more dangerous ones. The robber fly, for instance, looks like a bumblebee, and there's a caterpillar that can make its head look like it's a snake. She also adds that the coloring of the scarlet king snake, which is a nonvenomous snake, makes it resemble the venomous coral snake in appearance.

Actual Test 09

Question 1   p. 57

Sample Answer 1

Sports

1 love all sports
   - am not good at sports
   - would love to improve ability

2 sports = fun
   - often play them
   - would be great to play them better

Sample Response

If I had to choose between the two, I would go with sports over art. To begin with, I simply love all kinds of sports. I enjoy playing both team sports such as soccer and individual sports such as tennis and swimming. Unfortunately, I'm not very good at any of those sports. I try hard, but I'm not an athletic individual. So I'd love for my ability to play sports to improve. Secondly, sports are fun activities. I play them as often as I can after school and on the weekends. Since they are so enjoyable, it would be great if I could play them much better than I do at the present time. I think I would have even more fun if that were to happen.

Sample Answer 2

Art

1 like expressing self through art
   - art = hobby
   - not talented so want to get better

2 enjoy creating new things
   - could make art people like
   - make better representations of images in mind

Sample Response

It would be nice to play sports better, but I think being able to create better art would be a more interesting talent. Firstly, I like expressing myself through art. Art is one of my hobbies, so I paint, draw, and sketch. I'm not very talented though, so I wish I could be better. One of my friends is an excellent artist who makes amazing paintings, and I would love to be as good as she is. I also enjoy creating new things. If I were better at art, I would be able to make paintings, drawings, and sketches that people enjoy looking at. I would also be able to create better representations of the images in my mind, which would be a nice skill to have.

Question 2

p. 58

Listening Script

Now listen to two students discussing the announcement.

M Student: Check this out, Lucy. I just got my application for the International Business Internship Program. I'm so excited. I hope I get selected.

W Student: Yeah, uh, good luck.

M: Um . . . You don't sound too enthusiastic. I thought you'd be interested in this program as well since you're an Economics major.

W: You know, um, it sounds glamorous, but it seems like a totally unnecessary program.

M: In what way?

W: There are plenty of internship opportunities right here in the city. After all, more than a million people live in this area. There are plenty of local firms the school could help us get internships at.

M: But, uh . . . don't you want to go abroad? It's the chance of a lifetime.

W: Yes, that's true, but we're not a rich school. We simply don't have enough money to be sending so many students to places all around the planet. I wish the school would spend the money it has more wisely.

M: You make some good points, Lucy, but they're not going to stop me from applying. I still like the program.

Sample Answer

Reading Note
Summer internship program in Economics Department
- 10 top students
- intern in foreign countries
- unpaid but get $ for airfare, housing, and food

Listening Note
Woman → dislikes program

1 **internship opportunities in city**
   - 1 million people
   - can get internships at local firms

2 **school isn't rich**
   - doesn't have $ to send students abroad
   - should spend $ more wisely

Sample Response

The woman expresses her displeasure about the announcement by the Economics Department to the man. The Economics Department declares that it's going to start an international internship program for ten of its top students each summer. It will find internships in other countries and then provide airfare as well as housing and food costs for each student selected for the program. The woman dislikes this program very much despite the fact that her major is Economics. First, she remarks that the school shouldn't be sending students abroad since there are plenty of opportunities for the students to get internships in the city in which their school is located. Second, she points out that their school isn't wealthy, so it doesn't have much money. She wants the school to be more prudent with the money it has and to spend it better.

Question 3

p. 59

Listening Script

Now listen to a lecture on this topic in a biology class.

W Professor: We're all aware that parasites are harmful to their hosts. But did you know some parasites are capable of altering the behavior of their hosts . . . ? It's true. This phenomenon is called parasitic behavior alteration. Here are two examples . . .

Take a look at this . . . It's the spooked spider, which is found in Costa Rica. The spider is the prey of a parasitic wasp. Here's what happens . . . The wasp stings the spider and temporarily paralyzes it. Then, the wasp lays an egg in the spider's abdomen. The egg hatches, and a larva emerges. It feeds on the spider's blood while simultaneously injecting a chemical into the spider. After a few days, um, the chemical forces the spider to weave a web. Interestingly, the web isn't the normal design the spider makes but is something, um, radically different. Then, the larva kills the spider, consumes its blood, and uses the web as a cocoon for its pupa stage.

Here's another example . . . A parasite called *Toxoplasma gondii* uses rats as its host. Now, uh, rats are afraid of cats. That's no surprise since cats hunt them. Anyway, when the *Toxoplasma gondii* uses a rat as its host, the rat suddenly loses its fear of cats. As a result, the rat becomes easier for cats to catch and eat. Unfortunately for the cat, the parasite then moves into its body.

Sample Answer

Reading Note
Parasitic Behavior Alteration
parasitic behavior → harmful to host
- can force host to act atypically
- behavior may benefit parasite
- can cause death of host

Listening Note
Parasites → change behavior of hosts

1 **spooked spider**

- parasitic wasp preys on it
- stings spider → paralyzes → lays egg in spider
- egg hatches → larva feeds on spider's blood
- makes spider weave web → is different than normal
- kills spider → uses web as cocoon

2 rat
- parasite uses as host
- makes rats not be afraid of cats
- easy for cat to kill
- parasite gets into cats

Sample Response

The professor talks about how both spooked spiders and rats can be harmed by different parasites. First, she discusses the spooked spider. She notes that a type of wasp sometimes stings the spider and lays an egg in it. When the larva hatches, it injects a chemical into the spider that causes it to change its behavior. It makes a web that looks different from its normal one. After the larva kills the spider, it uses that web as a cocoon. Next, she discusses the rat. There is a parasite that affects some rats by making them no longer be afraid of cats. This makes it easier for cats to catch them, and then the parasite goes into the cat's body. Both examples are related to parasitic behavior alteration. This refers to how some parasites may cause their host to change its behavior. In some instances, the behavioral change kills the host.

Question 4

p. 60

Listening Script

Listen to part of a lecture in an environmental science class.

M Professor: Nowadays, the environment is a major concern for many people. Lots of the blame for various environmental problems has been placed on big businesses. Well, uh, nowadays, many of these businesses are trying to change their images so that people will regard them as being more ecofriendly corporations than they were in the past.

For instance, many companies are attempting to use more ecofriendly products. Retailers, um, you know, clothing stores, supermarkets, and other similar places, are switching from plastic bags to paper bags. Plastic bags have numerous disadvantages. Hmm . . . They don't degrade for many years, so they remain in landfills for a long time. They can be harmful to animals that get entangled in them or consume them, too. Paper bags, on the other hand, degrade quickly, cause hardly any problems for animals and the environment, and are made from renewable resources. So retailers switching to paper bags can tout that as a move

that's good for the environment.

Other businesses are making attempts to get their customers to help them reduce waste. For instance, some establishments that sell coffee, including Starbucks and Dunkin' Donuts, encourage people to bring their own mugs and other coffee containers when they purchase coffee. This is usually called something like Bring Your Own Mug. Some stores even offer discounts to customers who do that. That way, the stores can reduce the number of cups they use. This saves them money since they can buy fewer cups, and it also helps the environment. Most customers don't mind either since they can save a bit of money every time they buy coffee.

Sample Answer

Listening Note

Businesses changing images → more ecofriendly

1 use more ecofriendly products
- switch from plastic to paper bags
- plastic bags → degrade slowly and harm animals
- paper bags → degrade quickly, don't harm animals, and made from renewable resources

2 get customers to help reduce waste
- coffee shops → have customers bring own mugs
- reduces cups used
- saves money for customers

Sample Response

At the start of his lecture, the professor states that many companies are trying to become more ecofriendly since people have long thought of them as causing environmental problems. One way they're doing that is by using paper bags instead of plastic bags. The professor points out how plastic bags are bad for the environment in several ways. On the other hand, paper bags are much better for the environment. He notes that paper bags degrade very fast, don't hurt animals or the environment, and come from renewable resources. The next way some businesses are being ecofriendly is by having their customers assist them in reducing the amount of waste they produce. He mentions that places selling coffee such as Starbucks and Dunkin' Donuts ask their customers to bring their own coffee cups. They offer discounts to customers with cups, and they reduce the number of cups they use, which helps the environment.

Actual Test 10

p. 63
Question 1

Sample Answer 1

Agree

1 **understand topic better when talk about it**
   - history class
   - learned topic better thanks to discussion

2 **give and take between students = more learning**
   - student challenges opinion → defend argument
   - must think more about topic

Sample Response

I believe this statement is correct because students clearly learn more when they participate in class discussions. I'm currently a student, and several of my classes have weekly discussions. I have noticed that when I get the opportunity to talk about a certain topic, I understand it better. This happened to me in my history class last week. We had a discussion about the causes of World War II. When I got the chance to talk about it in class, the topic became so much clearer to me. In addition, the give and take that goes on between students helps us all learn. When another student challenges my opinion, I have to defend my argument. This makes me think more about the topic, so I learn it better.

Sample Answer 2

Disagree

1 **students who speak = no idea about topic**
   - two students in science discussion
   - made many mistakes

2 **I never speak in discussions**
   - still get all A's
   - am shy so don't like speaking in front of others

Sample Response

I wish it were true that students learn more when they participate in class discussions, but I believe this statement is incorrect. My teachers enjoy having the students participate in class discussions, but it seems like the students that speak the most have no idea what they're talking about. In a recent discussion in my science class, the two students who dominated the discussion made several obvious mistakes. It was clear that they weren't learning anything, and neither were the students who had to hear them speak. Another thing is that I never participate in class discussions, yet I get all A's in my classes. I'm shy, so I dislike speaking in front of others. Nevertheless, this hasn't

prevented me from learning the material as my high grades prove.

p. 64
Question 2

Listening Script

Now listen to two students discussing the announcement.

W Student: Oh, no. This is awful news. I may have to reconsider my plans to live in Morrison Hall next year.

M Student: Ah, you read the announcement that the lounges are being converted to kitchens, didn't you?

W: I just found out. I couldn't disagree more with what the student housing office is doing.

M: Out of curiosity, why do you oppose this decision?

W: Off the top of my head, I can think of two reasons. The first, uh, is that most of the students in Morrison Hall love hanging out in the lounges. They're popular places to socialize and also to do work.

M: That's true. I spend lots of time with my friends there, and I don't even live in Morrison Hall.

W: Yeah, I do the same.

M: And the other reason?

W: Imagine, uh, thirty students trying to share kitchen facilities that small. They'll be fighting over who gets to cook food at various times. And there are bound to be arguments if someone is using too much space in the refrigerator or freezer.

M: You're right. It sounds like it's going to be a disaster.

Sample Answer

Reading Note
Morrison Hall lounges will be changed
- will become kitchens
- will be equipped with cooking facilities

Listening Note
Woman → dislikes decision

1 **lounges popular**
   - students socialize in them
   - do work there

2 **kitchen facilities small**
   - students must share
   - will argue about cooking and using refrigerator and freezer

Sample Response

The woman and the man have a conversation in which they discuss the announcement that was made by the student housing office. It mentions that the largest dormitory on campus is going to be closed during the summer in order for it to be renovated. The school is going to change all of the lounges in the dormitory into kitchens, which will allow the students living there to cook for themselves. The woman considers this a terrible decision and mentions that she might no longer wish to live in that dormitory next year. She points out that the lounges in the dormitory are extremely popular for socializing and studying. She comments that she spends time in those lounges despite not even living in that dormitory. Then, she says that there are surely going to be arguments between students concerning the usage of the kitchen facilities. Since they'll be so small, students are likely to fight over how they can use the kitchens.

Question 3

Listening Script

Now listen to a lecture on this topic in a marketing class.

M Professor: I once believed that infomercials were pointless. You know what I'm talking about, don't you . . . ? I'm referring to those long commercials you often see on late-night television during which a person demonstrates how to use some kind of product to convince you to buy it.

Well, let me tell you a personal story. A few months ago, I was watching television with my children. Somehow, we wound up watching an infomercial for an ice cream maker that lets you make your own ice cream at home. My two sons got excited because they love ice cream. They asked me to buy it, but, well, I didn't want to. After all, I figured, the machine must be too complicated to use.

Anyway, the person hosting the infomercial started explaining how to use the machine. She mixed some ingredients, poured them into the ice cream maker, and then set the controls. Do you know what . . . ? It was much simpler than I'd imagined. By the time the infomercial ended ten minutes later, I was sold. I could practically taste the ice cream. I picked up the phone and called the number on the screen. And guess what . . . The infomercial was right. The machine was easy to use. If it hadn't been for that infomercial, I never would have purchased an ice cream maker.

Sample Answer

Reading Note
Product Demonstrations

products look complex or hard to operate or understand
- conduct product demonstrations
- show how easy product is to use
- can do in stores, on streets, or on TV

Listening Note

Infomercials → long commercials on TV

saw infomercial for ice cream maker
- sons wanted to buy
- professor thought was too complicated

infomercial explained how to use
- was very simple
- ordered ice cream maker

Sample Response

The professor tells his class about a story involving him and his two sons. One day, they were watching television together, and they saw an infomercial. According to the reading passage, companies use infomercials, which are product demonstrations, to show people how to use their products. The reason they make infomercials is that some customers may believe their products are too complicated or difficult to use. By conducting product demonstrations, companies can show viewers exactly how to use their products and therefore prove that they aren't hard to use. That's exactly what happened to the professor. He watched an infomercial for an ice cream maker. His sons asked him to buy it, but he didn't want to because he was convinced that making ice cream would be too hard. Yet after the infomercial concluded, he realized how easy it is to make ice cream, so he ordered an ice cream maker for his family.

Question 4

Listening Script

Listen to part of a lecture in a biology class.

W Professor: Animals migrate for a variety of reasons. The two most common ones are to search for food sources and to go to their traditional breeding grounds. Unfortunately for these animals, human development repeatedly encroaches upon their migratory paths. But people have devised ways to assist some animals.

Many species of fish, including salmon, return to their birthplaces to breed. These places are typically far inland in rivers and streams. When dams are built across these rivers and streams, the salmon are unable to swim upstream though. As a result, they cannot reproduce. However, people solved this problem by building fish ladders on rivers and streams that were obstructed by dams. These fish ladders help salmon and other species easily move upstream and downstream. Here's a picture . . .
Notice that there's a series of steps filled with water. You can see how the fish leap from step to step to bypass the dam. There are actually many types of fish ladders . . . not just the one I've shown you . . . but the purpose of each of them is to help fish get past dams.

Actual Test 10 **25**

On land, highways represent dangerous obstacles for animals attempting to get from one side of the road to the other. I'm sure you've all seen dead animals, uh, you know, road kill, by the side of the road that were hit by cars or trucks. Well, one way to prevent needless deaths is to build underpasses. These are tunnels going beneath roads. By using these underpasses, animals can avoid being hit by vehicles. And, uh, yes, these animals actually do use the underpasses. If you watch some videos, you can see various species of animals safely passing through them.

Sample Answer

Listening Note

Animal migration → interfered with by humans

1 **dams → cause problems for fish such as salmon**
   - can't swim upstream
   - fish ladders → help fish move upstream
   - leap from one step to another

2 **highways → animals killed crossing them**
   - build underpasses → tunnels beneath roads
   - animals use them → don't get hit

Sample Response

The professor lectures that animals often migrate to find food and to get to their breeding grounds. She says that human development sometimes interferes with migrating animals, but then she describes two ways in which people help animals as they migrate. The first way is the fish ladder. Fish ladders are found by dams that are blocking rivers and streams. Fish such as salmon, which swim up rivers and streams in order to reproduce, use fish ladders to get around dams. By using the fish ladders, they are able to get to their breeding grounds and reproduce. The second way the professor mentions is that people build underpasses beneath busy roads. She says that lots of animals get killed when they get hit by vehicles as they try to cross the road. However, when people build underpasses, animals can safely cross roads by going beneath them through tunnels. This lets animals avoid getting killed as they migrate.

Question 1 p. 69

Sample Answer 1

Advantages

1 **home = costs nothing**
   - friends don't have much money
   - hang out at someone's home

2 **many activities at home**
   - play computer games + watch videos

Disadvantages

1 **live w/parents → hard to socialize**
   - parents won't let friends stay after 10 P.M.

2 **person's roommates & friends → don't get along**
   - brother's housemates dislike friends
   - uncomfortable to socialize at home

Sample Response

Let me discuss the advantages of socializing at home. First, it doesn't cost anything to spend time at home. My friends and I don't have much money, so we almost always hang out together at someone's home. There are also many activities to do at a person's home. My friends and I love playing computer games and watching videos at our homes. Regarding the disadvantages, people who live with their parents can have problems socializing at home. For example, my parents won't let my friends stay over past ten at night. A second disadvantage is that people's roommates and friends don't always get along. My brother has two housemates, and they dislike his friends, so it's uncomfortable for him to socialize with his friends at home.

Sample Answer 2

Advantages

1 **countless places to go**
   - restaurants, coffee shops, & parks

2 **can be active if not at home**
   - rollerblade, play soccer, & do other activities = active + healthy

Disadvantages

1 **expensive**
   - friends have debt from socializing outside home

2 **travel time**
   - hard to travel 1 hour to meet friends

There are several benefits and drawbacks to socializing at places other than homes. One benefit is that there are countless places to go. My friends and I socialize at restaurants, coffee shops, and parks. An additional benefit is that people can be active if they aren't at home. Several of my friends socialize by rollerblading at parks, playing soccer, and doing other similar activities. They can therefore socialize and be active and healthy. On the other hand, the primary drawback is that socializing like that is expensive. Some of my friends have gotten into debt by constantly socializing outside their homes. Another problem is that going to other places requires traveling time. I'm busy, so it's hard to travel somewhere for one hour just to meet my friends.

Question 2

Listening Script

Now listen to two students discussing the announcement.

M Student: I'm pleased to see the school is going to open an office to assist students with living off campus.

W Student: So am I. It's too bad this is my senior year though. I could have used some assistance from an office like that a couple of years ago.

M: You're telling me.

W: Why do you support it? You've always lived on campus.

M: That's true. But I'm thinking of the benefits to the student body as a whole. I mean, uh, there isn't enough room on campus for every student here, and there aren't plans to build any new dorms.

W: That's right.

M: So lots of students have no choice but to live off campus. They need professional advice at some times. This office will hopefully provide it.

W: I sure hope so.

M: Freshmen especially need assistance. Think about it . . . Teenagers come here from out of state and then have to live off campus. Lots of them get, um, ripped off. An off-campus living office should help prevent that.

W: I believe you're right.

Sample Answer

Reading Note

Off-campus living office to open
- will provide advice for students
- help students find housing
- inform them of average rents

Listening Note

Man → likes decision

1 not enough housing on campus
- some students must live off campus
- could use professional advice

2 freshmen need help
- are teens from out of state
- get ripped off
- office can help prevent that

Sample Response

The man and the woman discuss an announcement by the school administration. The announcement reads that the school is going to open an office to assist students that live off campus. The employees at the office will provide this assistance for students in a variety of ways. The man strongly supports this new office and believes that opening it will be beneficial to a large number of students at the school. He points out that there is not enough dormitory space on campus for all of the students, so some students have no choice but to live off campus. He believes the advice the office can provide them will be helpful. He also declares that many freshmen from faraway places get stuck living off campus. He wants them to avoid getting ripped off by landlords, and he feels that this office will accomplish that goal.

Question 3

Listening Script

Now listen to a lecture on this topic in an environmental science class.

M Professor: I know many people love talking about global warming these days, but, interestingly enough, the world has typically been much colder than it currently is. In fact, in the past fifty thousand years or so, ice ages have been, um, far more prevalent than warm weather. Thus we should be discussing global cooling rather than global warming.

There are times when global cooling can be triggered for only a year or two. This sometimes happens because of volcanic eruptions. For instance, in 1815, Mount Tambora, a volcano in Indonesia, erupted. It was one of the most powerful eruptions in recorded history. Volcanic ash soared high into the stratosphere and got caught up in the air currents there. Then, the ash began traveling around the world.

This was when the problems began. You see, um, the ashes in the stratosphere reflected sunlight, which made global temperatures drop. The next year was called "The Year without a Summer." The effects of the Tambora eruption were mostly felt in the Northern Hemisphere. It was so cold that it snowed in August in the United States and Europe. Winter came early, so many crops failed. Famine was widespread, and hundreds of thousands of people died. Fortunately, global temperatures later rose, but that short period of global cooling was devastating to people in countries all around the world.

Sample Answer

Reading Note

Global Cooling = Earth's average temp. declines

- polar ice caps expand
- temperate zones → colder
- glaciers extend
- species die out
- can happen due to natural phenomena

Listening Note

Volcanic eruption → can cause global cooling

Mount Tambora erupted in 1815

- powerful eruption
- ash into stratosphere → spread around the world

The Year without a Summer

- snowed in August
- crops failed
- famine
- 100,000s of people died

Sample Response

In his lecture, the professor describes to his class what happened when Mount Tambora erupted in 1815. According to him, the volcanic eruption was extremely powerful, and it shot ash high into the atmosphere. Then, the ash began to move around the world. There was so much ash in the sky that it reflected sunlight, so temperatures around the world went down. This caused global cooling. Global cooling is a phenomenon involving the declining of temperatures around the world. It can be caused by natural events, such as volcanic eruptions. There are several negative effects of it. These include many species dying and the polar caps and glaciers expanding. The year after the Tambora eruption was called "The Year without a Summer." It snowed in August, many crops failed, and lots of people died. All of these negative effects were due to the global cooling that was caused by the volcano.

Question 4

p. 72

Listening Script

Listen to part of a lecture in a sociology class.

W Professor: How many of you took the commuter train to school today . . . ? Okay, it looks like about, hmm . . . about a quarter of you. I did that as well even though I own a car. Actually, I hardly ever drive to work. The commuter train is simply too convenient, especially for people who live in the suburbs. Trains running from suburbs to downtown areas provide numerous benefits for both people and the environment. Let me tell you how . . .

Like me, many people who work in cities don't live there. For one thing, the costs of housing and rent are way more expensive downtown than they are in the suburbs. When metropolitan areas have commuter trains, which provide a fast, cheap, and traffic-free way to get downtown, more people can live in suburbs, where the quality of life is generally better. Thus millions of people in places all around the world benefit with regard to their working and living arrangements.

Commuter trains help the environment in several ways, too. By taking the train, I don't have to drive my car or take a bus. Both types of vehicles use internal combustion engines that pump pollution into the air in vast quantities. When people eschew cars and buses in favor of commuter trains, they're helping protect the environment. In addition, with fewer cars and buses on the roads, traffic flows at a faster rate. This enables drivers to save gas since they can make their trips faster and don't have to sit idly in traffic. Thus gasoline, a valuable natural resource, is saved, and less pollution is released since the cars' engines are running for less time.

Sample Answer

Listening Note

Commuter train → convenient for people in suburbs

1 **people work in cities but don't live there**
   - housing $ too much
   - commuter trains → fast, cheap, and traffic-free way downtown

2 **commuter trains = good for environment**
   - can avoid driving car or taking bus → makes less pollution
   - fewer cars and buses on roads → traffic moves faster
   - can save gasoline since fewer cars idle in traffic

Sample Response

The professor lectures about commuter trains and mentions that they have many benefits. She identifies commuter trains as those which run from downtown areas to nearby suburbs. First, the professor comments that many people live in suburbs but work downtown. They can do that because they take commuter trains to work. By living in suburbs, people can spend less on housing, have a better quality of life, and get to their workplaces both quickly and cheaply. Second, she comments that commuter trains can help the environment in a number of ways. She points out that when people drive cars or take buses, their vehicles release lots of pollution. So when they take commuter trains, they aren't polluting the air. Additionally, when fewer people are driving, traffic is lighter, so drivers make their commutes faster. That further prevents more harmful emissions from being released into the atmosphere.

Actual Test 12

Question 1

Sample Answer 1

Homework Assignments

1 **homework concerns class material**
   - math homework is about info in class
   - grade students → determine who knows material

2 **review material**
   - don't always understand lecture
   - do homework → material makes sense

Sample Response

Teachers can evaluate their students better by giving them daily homework assignments to submit than by grading them on class discussions. To begin with, most homework deals with the material a teacher covered in class. For instance, math homework is always about the math problems the students learned to solve. By grading students on how well they complete that homework, teachers can determine who understands the material and who doesn't. Another benefit of daily homework is that students can review the information that they learned in class. Sometimes I don't always understand a teacher's lecture. However, when I do the homework, the material I learn in class suddenly makes sense to me. For me, that's a major benefit of doing daily homework assignments.

Sample Answer 2

Class Discussions

1 **shows who knows material**

   - no time to check notes or books
   - students who give good responses know the material

2 **good students participate**
   - make comments during discussions
   - bad students stay quiet

Sample Response

Teachers ought to evaluate their students by grading them according to how well they participate during class discussions rather than by grading them on their homework assignments. During class discussions, students don't have time to check their notes or to read their books. Instead, they have to give instant responses. The students who can do this clearly know the material well whereas the ones who can't do this don't know the information. Additionally, in my experience, good students participate in class discussions while bad ones say absolutely nothing. We have weekly discussions in my history class. The good students all make comments during the discussion, but the bad ones are quiet. The teacher can therefore grade the students according to who speaks and who doesn't.

Question 2

Listening Script

Now listen to two students discussing the announcement.

W Student: Is this some kind of a horrible joke?

M Student: Er . . . What are you referring to?

W: The community service announcement. Have you heard about it?

M: Sure. You don't like it?

W: I loathe it. I'm going to graduate next semester, but now I've got to do community service in addition to writing a thesis and trying to find a job? That's so unfair.

M: Personally, I happen to like the announcement.

W: Huh?

M: Well, in addition to getting to help our neighbors, it can help us, too. My cousin volunteered at a hospital one summer. It changed her life. After working there, she changed her major from Economics and attended medical school. She's a doctor today.

W: That's good for her, but how will it help me?

M: You said you're looking for a job, right? If you volunteer at a place you want to work at, you'll have an advantage.

W: In what way?

M: The people you volunteer with will get to know you. If there's a permanent job position open and you work hard, they'll probably consider you over the other applicants.

Actual Test 12   29

Reading Note

Students must do community service

- do 16 hours/semester
- can't graduate unless volunteer

Listening Note

Man → approves of decision

1 can help volunteers
- cousin volunteered at hospital
- decided to become a doctor thanks to experience

2 have advantage by volunteering
- people at place volunteer get to know students
- if job position opens, have better chance to get job

Sample Response

The man and the woman discuss the announcement by the dean of students that all students at the school have to do volunteer work starting in the spring semester. According to it, any students who don't do enough community service won't be allowed to graduate. The man supports the decision by the dean of students and believes it's a good idea to obligate all of the students to do community service. Firstly, he claims that doing it can help change a person's life. As an example, he mentions that his cousin volunteered at a hospital once and decided to become a doctor thanks to her experience there. Next, he advises the woman that she should volunteer at a place where she might like to work. By working hard there, she could become the frontrunner for any jobs that become available at the workplace at which she volunteers.

Question 3

p. 77

Listening Script

Now listen to a lecture on this topic in an education class.

M Professor: How do we learn . . . ? Well, first, we learn simple things. After all, you can't do complex tasks until you learn to do basic ones first, right? Here, uh, allow me to give you some examples from the academic and, um, nonacademic worlds.

Think about when you first attended school. What did you learn . . . ? That's right. Among the first things you learned were numbers and the alphabet. Once you learned those two basic things, you were able to build upon that knowledge, weren't you? For instance, after learning to count, you subsequently studied basic math such as addition and subtraction. Knowing them let you learn multiplication, division, and more difficult mathematical concepts. As for learning the alphabet, well, once you did

that, you started reading words and sentences, and you also became able to write. Do you see how transfer of learning works?

Now, um, what about nonacademic learning? Let me think . . . Most of you probably learned to ride a bike when you were young. Later, that knowledge helped you learn how to drive a car. Uh, I'm assuming most of you have your driver's licenses, of course. What else . . . ? Well, if you wanted to learn to drive a bus or a truck, you'd have some basic knowledge to rely upon. You see, uh, you build upon the basic knowledge you have to learn more complicated things.

Reading Note

The Transfer of Learning

- learn one thing → leads to more knowledge
- new knowledge = harder or more complicated
- essential learning method

Listening Note

Learn basic tasks and then complex ones

1 academic examples
- learn to count → learn + and - → learn ×, ÷, and other math
- learn alphabet → read words and sentences → write

2 nonacademic example
- learn to ride bike
- then learn to drive
- if want, can learn to drive bus or truck

Sample Response

During his lecture, the professor provides some examples of academic and nonacademic learning. First, he discusses academic learning. He says that two of the first things students learned at school were numbers and the alphabet. After the students knew how to do them, they learned more difficult information. For instance, the students learned to solve math problems after learning to count. And they became able to read and write once they became familiar with the alphabet. As for nonacademic learning, he says most of them probably learned to ride a bike at an early age. Later, they learned how to drive a car, which is more complicated. He points out that they could use that knowledge if they decided to learn how to drive a bus or truck, too. These examples are related to the transfer of learning. According to it, people learn easy things and then use that knowledge to learn information that's more difficult or complicated.

Question 4

p. 78

Listening Script

Listen to part of a lecture in a zoology class.

W Professor: Many animals form social groups. We have different names for them, such as, uh, herd for land animals, school for fish, and flock for birds. Animals form both family groups and nonfamily groups. Family groups are like lion prides, in which every animal is related in some way. Nonfamily groups are like the massive herds of zebras wandering in Africa. In nonfamily groups, the majority of the animals are unrelated. There are two main reasons animals form social groups: to find food . . . and to provide protection from predators.

Many animals forage and hunt for food in groups since there are a few advantages to doing so. For example, groups have more eyes to search for food and more animals to help kill or gather food. Predators like lions and wolves hunt in groups, which enables them to bring down large animals they would almost never be able to kill all by themselves. Dolphins are known to work in teams to attack schools of fish so that they can feed well. And flocks of birds can more easily spot food sources when flying together than when flying as individuals.

Social groups offer protection for animals as well. Large land animals such as the wildebeest and water buffalo can form protective walls around their young and thwart attacks by predators. Birds flying in a fast-moving flock that quickly changes directions represent hard targets for hawks and eagles to penetrate to pick off individual birds. And many animals, including the African meerkat and North American prairie dog, post sentries to watch for approaching predators. The sentries give warnings so that members of the groups can flee to their underground lairs when predators approach.

Sample Answer

Listening Note

Animals form family and nonfamily social groups

1 **find food**
   - large groups = more eyes to find food and more animals to kill prey
   - lions and wolves → hunt in groups to kill large animals
   - dolphins → attack schools of fish
   - birds → easily spot food sources when in flocks

2 **protection**
   - wildebeest and water buffalo → protect young
   - bird flocks → harder for hawks and eagles to attack them in groups
   - meerkat and prairie dog → post sentries to watch for predators

Sample Response

The professor discusses the social groups that animals form. She says they may be family or nonfamily groups. According to the professor, the first reason animals form social groups is to obtain food more easily. She gives several examples of how animals do this. She states that lions and wolves work together to kill large animals that they can't kill alone. She mentions how dolphins catch fish in groups, and she says that birds look for food in flocks since it's easier to find if many birds are looking at the same time. The second reason animals establish social groups is to protect themselves from predators. Again, she provides many examples. Large animals like the water buffalo can form circles around their young to keep predators away from them. Birds can protect themselves from eagles and hawks by flying in flocks. And some animals even post sentries that alert other animals if danger is approaching.

Actual Test 13

Question 1

p. 81

Sample Answer 1

Receive a Gift

1 **person puts thought into present**
   - is personal touch
   - birthday → friends gave thoughtful presents

2 **can be pleasantly surprised**
   - friend gave me earrings
   - wasn't expecting → made me happy

Sample Response

When it's my birthday, I'm much happier when I receive gifts as opposed to money. For starters, when a person takes the time to buy a gift, that individual puts some thought into the present. I really appreciate that kind of personal touch. At my birthday party four months ago, several friends gave me very thoughtful presents. I really loved the fact that they cared enough to buy something special for me. Another benefit of receiving gifts is that you can be pleasantly surprised when receiving something unexpected. For instance, my best friend gave me some earrings she had previously seen me checking out at a jewelry store. I totally wasn't expecting to get them, and it made me so happy when she gave them to me.

Receive Money

1 avoid getting gift you can't use
- aunt gave me sweater
- too small → can't wear

2 can purchase something you want
- got several gifts of $ for birthday
- bought new bicycle

Sample Response

I'm much happier when I receive money than when I receive presents for my birthday. By giving you money, a person can avoid buying you a gift you can't use. My aunt gave me a sweater for my last birthday. Unfortunately, it was too small, so I couldn't wear it. Basically, she wasted her money by purchasing a completely useless gift for me. Additionally, when a person gives you money for your birthday, it gives you the opportunity to purchase something you actually want. And if you get multiple gifts of money, you can combine the presents to buy yourself something really nice. I received several gifts of money for my last birthday, so I bought a new bicycle for myself. That was a great birthday gift.

Question 2

p. 82

Listening Script

Now listen to two students discussing the letter.

M Student: The student who wrote this letter makes a good point. The parking situation here on campus is atrocious.

W Student: I've heard some people say that. My roommate, for instance, uh, always complains that she can't find a parking spot near the dorm. But, well . . .

M: Well what?

W: Well . . . I don't agree with his suggestion. I don't want the school to build a parking lot behind Miller Hall.

M: But it would be an ideal place for a parking garage.

W: True. Yet lots of students hang out in that area. It's a nice shaded place with lots of trees. I frequently go there with my friends to hang out and also to study.

M: I wasn't aware of that.

W: You should go there sometime. It's really nice. And another thing . . .

M: Yes?

W: It seems to me that there's enough parking on campus. It's merely not conveniently located. So I think the letter writer should do the same thing I always tell my roommate.

M: Which is?

W: Walk. Getting a little exercise won't hurt.

Reading Note

Unhappy w/parking situation
- make new parking lot
- use area behind Miller Hall

Listening Note

Woman → disagrees w/letter writer

1 no parking lot behind Miller Hall
- students hang out in area
- study there, too

2 is enough parking on campus
- is not conveniently located
- but can park and then walk

Sample Response

The two students discuss the letter to the editor written by a student. In the letter, the student encourages the school to improve the parking situation on campus. He advises the school to use the empty area behind Miller Hall to construct a new parking lot. The woman tells the man that she disagrees with the student's suggestion. The first reason she feels this way is that she and many other students enjoy spending time in that area. She says it's a nice place with many trees, and students enjoy studying and socializing there. The second reason she feels this way is that she believes the school doesn't lack parking spots. Instead, she believes the parking spots are in poor locations. She tells the man that the students can simply park their cars and then walk to wherever on campus they are going.

Question 3

p. 83

Listening Script

Now listen to a lecture on this topic in a biology class.

W Professor: Depending on where they grow and the sort of terrain they live in, plants have different energy needs. All plants must utilize energy for three major areas: growth . . . maintenance . . . and reproduction. Let's examine how both annuals and perennials balance their energy expenditures.

Annuals are plants that live for a single growing season and then die. Therefore, uh, growth and reproduction are of great importance to them. At the beginning of the growing season, virtually all of the energy which annuals use is directed toward growth. After all, um, they must grow and mature before reproducing. Then, near the ends of their life cycles, annuals direct most of their energy toward reproduction. They must develop seeds and have those seeds germinate so that new plants can begin to grow at the start of the next year. During the short life cycles of annuals, the maintenance of their roots, stems, leaves, and flowers is secondary to growth and reproduction.

Perennials, such as trees, live for more than two years. Thus, uh, they expend much more energy on maintenance, especially if they're growing in harsh environments with extreme temperatures and weather. Since perennials are long-lived plants, they must maintain themselves for many years. Growth therefore comes in second in energy usage while reproduction is last. Perennials expend energy on reproduction only in short bursts each season.

Sample Answer

Reading Note

The Principle of Allocation

organisms employ energy efficiently
- need energy for many things
- effectively manage the energy used for each thing
- less energy → less important tasks
- more energy → more important tasks

Listening Note

Plants balance energy for growth, maintenance, and reproduction

1 **annuals**
   - most energy on growth at first
   - more energy on reproduction at ends of lives
   - less energy on maintenance

2 **perennials**
   - more energy on maintenance
   - growth → is secondary
   - reproduction → last

Sample Response

The professor lectures on how annuals and perennials expend energy. She mentions that all plants need to spend energy in the three major areas of growth, maintenance, and reproduction. She remarks that annuals, which live for one year, spend most of their energy on growth. Then, before dying, they expend energy on reproduction, which ensures that new annuals will grow during the next year. She also points out that annuals use little energy on maintenance. On the other hand, perennials, which are plants that live for more than two years, spend a great deal of their energy on maintenance since they live for so long. They spend less energy on growth and much less on reproduction. The actions of these two plants both relate to the principle of allocation. This involves how organisms utilize the limited amount of energy they possess. They spend more energy on important tasks and less energy on less important ones.

Question 4
p. 84

Listening Script

Listen to part of a lecture in an anthropology class.

M Professor: Anthropologists believe that the horse was tamed somewhere in modern-day Kazakhstan, which is in Asia, around 4000 B.C. Though it took time for domestication to spread to other lands, the benefits of having tame horses were readily apparent to people in ancient times. There are two major ways that the domestication of the horse changed society in the past.

Thousands of years ago, the main method of power used by humans was their own muscle power. But, um, after the horse was domesticated, that changed. Horses started being used as beasts of burden and farm animals. They were capable of carrying heavy loads great distances. This improved trade contacts between people living far from one another. When used on farms, horses could plow the land and do other jobs. This, in turn, enabled farmers to break more ground and to plant more crops. By producing more food, populations increased, and civilization was able to begin.

Horses also changed the face of warfare. They enabled large armies to move great distances. One of the greatest examples of this is the Mongol armies, whose soldiers rode on horseback and traveled all the way to Europe from their homeland in East Asia in the thirteenth century. Generals in ancient times, such as Alexander the Great, and leaders in more recent times, such as Napoleon Bonaparte, used cavalry, uh, soldiers on horseback, to win great victories. Horses allowed armies to move fast and to bring large numbers of soldiers to decisive points on battlefields, where they could deliver shock attacks. It wasn't until the twentieth century, when tanks and trucks began to be used, that horses were phased out of armies.

Sample Answer

Listening Note

Domestication of horse → benefitted people

1 **power source**
   - could carry heavy loads
   - could plow land on farms → more crops

2 **warfare**
   - let armies move great distances → Mongols
   - soldiers on horseback → Alexander the Great and Napoleon

Sample Response

The professor tells the students that the horse was first domesticated in Asia around 6,000 years ago. It had a profound influence on society in two primary ways. The first way was that the horse provided a source of power other than human power. Merchants used horses to carry heavy loads, so they could trade with people far from them. Farmers used horses to till the land and to do various chores. Thanks to horses, farmers could grow more crops, so people ate better, and they were able to establish civilization. The second major way horses affected society concerned war. By riding on horses, armies such as the Mongols could ride vast distances. The professor also mentions Alexander the Great and Napoleon as generals who used cavalry effectively. According to the professor, it wasn't until the 1900s that armies stopped using horses in battle.

Actual Test 14

Question 1
p. 87

Sample Answer 1

Agree

1 **students too shy to volunteer**
   - teacher calls on them → answer
   - best friend is shy but speaks if teacher asks ?

2 **teachers must teach all students**
   - don't just teach good students
   - encourage all students to talk

Sample Response

I strongly agree with the statement that teachers ought to encourage their students to speak when they are having class discussions. There are many students who want to speak, but they are too shy to volunteer their thoughts. However, if the teacher calls on them, they will gladly contribute to the discussion. My best friend is like that. She never raises her hand to talk in class because she's shy, but she'll speak up every time the teacher asks her a direct question. Another thing is that teachers need to teach to the entire class, not just to the few students who enjoy speaking. Therefore teachers need to encourage all students, both the good and the bad ones, to give their thoughts and ideas during class discussions.

Sample Answer 2

Disagree

1 **some students uncomfortable**
   - get nervous or scared

   - I stutter → look silly when speaking

2 **discussions get ruined when all talk**
   - not all students have something to say
   - just let students who want to talk speak

Sample Response

I disagree with the statement because I don't think it's necessary for teachers to encourage their students to speak during class discussions. First and foremost, some students feel uncomfortable speaking in front of others, so teachers shouldn't try to make these students do something that makes them nervous or scared. I get nervous speaking in front of other people, so I don't talk during discussions. I hate when my teacher calls on me to give my thoughts because I start stuttering and end up looking silly in front of everyone else. Second of all, class discussions get ruined when the teacher makes every student speak. Not every student has something interesting to say. Instead, teachers should let the students who want to contribute speak while the others simply listen.

Question 2
p. 88

Listening Script

Now listen to two students discussing the announcement.

W Student: Chris, what do you think of the ways the school is going to try to save money by reducing the amount of electricity it uses?

M Student: I fully support what the school's doing.

W: Can you tell me why?

M: Sure. There are two primary reasons.

W: Which are . . . ?

M: The first is simple: The school is using too much electricity, and energy costs are, uh, they're skyrocketing these days. By using less electricity, the school can save money. Then, it can spend the money on other things.

W: Like what?

M: Hmm . . . Perhaps it could buy some more laboratory equipment or fund some scholarships. Either one would be nice.

W: Yeah, that makes sense to me.

M: The second reason concerns the heating of the buildings.

W: Personally, I'm worried about that. I don't want to freeze while I'm trying to learn in class.

M: Then wear a jacket. That's what I'm planning to do. Plus, it doesn't really get that cold here during winter, so I don't have a problem with how the school intends to heat the classrooms.

Reading Note

School to reduce electricity usage

- heat in academic buildings turned off during part of day
- lights in unused classrooms turned off at night

Listening Note

Man → agrees w/decision

1 **use less electricity → spend $ on other things**
   - buy lab equipment
   - fund scholarships

2 **not concerned about heating in rooms**
   - wear jacket
   - doesn't get too cold in winter

Sample Response

The man talks to the woman about the announcement that was made by the Building and Grounds Department. In an effort to save both electricity and money, the school is going to heat its academic buildings for a limited number of hours each day. Additionally, the school will turn off the lights in all of its empty classrooms at night. The man supports the school in its effort to reduce the usage of electricity. The first comment he makes is that the school will be able to save a large amount of money, which it can then use to pay for scholarships, equipment, or other things. The second comment he makes is that students who are cold can simply wear jackets when they're in class. He believes the winter weather in the region isn't very cold, so it shouldn't be a problem for the school to heat the buildings less often.

Question 3

p. 89

Listening Script

Now listen to a lecture on this topic in an education class.

W Professor: As future educators, it's imperative that you learn to handle classroom behavior. After all, um, part of your job will be making sure your students learn to behave properly. Let me tell you what happened to me in the past . . .

When I taught elementary school students, I had one boy that was quite rambunctious. He always hit other students and disrupted both class and playtime. One day, I found him crying outside. I asked him what the problem was, and he responded that he had no friends and that everyone hated him. I told him he could make friends simply by being nicer to others. The possibility of having friends seemed to hearten him, so he improved his behavior, um, dramatically. Pretty soon, he was friends with several students.

Another year, I had a girl who thought she was, uh, the queen of the classroom or something. She bossed the other students around and tried to make them do everything for her. She wouldn't even listen to me at times. Everyone in the class strongly disliked her. I tried advising her to change her behavior, but she wouldn't listen to me. By the end of the year, she was miserable. She didn't fit in with the other students, and they wanted nothing to do with her and her bad attitude.

Reading Note

Social Skills for Children

social skills → kids learn from parents, teachers, and peers
- learn to get along w/others
- good social skills = popular kid
- bad social skills = ostracized kid

Listening Note

Students must learn good behavior

1 **rambunctious boy**
   - caused many problems
   - was crying → said others hated him
   - told him to be nicer
   - improved behavior → became friends w/students

2 **bossy girl**
   - ordered others around
   - advised her to change → didn't listen
   - miserable at end of year
   - other students wanted nothing to do w/her

Sample Response

The professor tells the students they need to learn how to handle classroom behavior as teachers and then provides two examples from her past. She mentions a boy who used to hit students and cause various problems. Later, the boy complained that he had no friends and felt bad about that. The professor advised the boy to be nicer to others. The boy changed his behavior and soon had some friends. The professor also mentions a girl who was very bossy and often ordered the other students around. Despite the professor's advice to change, the girl wouldn't. As a result, the other students wouldn't do anything with her, and that made the girl very unhappy. Both incidents are related to social skills for children in that students need to learn how to behave well while they're around others. If they don't act properly, they will be disliked by their peers and won't have any friends.

Question 4

p. 90

Listening Script

Listen to part of a lecture in a zoology class.

M Professor: A savannah is a type of biome with wide-open grasslands and few trees. Savannahs can be found in Africa, Australia, India, and South America. One common characteristic of a savannah is that it has alternating dry and wet seasons. The scarcity of water during parts of the year means that most of the vegetation dries out and is near death until the rains return. With supplies of food and water never a sure thing, animals living in savannahs have had to adapt in various ways.

One adaptation method is that they, uh, they migrate to where food and water are located. The Serengeti, which is located in Eastern Africa, has enormous herds of animals, including zebras and wildebeests, that migrate to find sustenance. Every year in Tanzania and Kenya in the late spring and summer months, the largest animal migration in the world takes place. Several million mammals belonging to many different species move north around 800 kilometers to find better grasslands and more water. A few months later, they migrate again when the weather changes.

Other animals find ways to get enough water during the dry season. The elephant is perhaps the best example of an animal that has effectively adapted to the savannah's dry season. Elephants can find water in trees and dry riverbeds. The baobab tree can hold large amounts of water, even, uh, even during the dry season. Elephants use their tusks and trunks to dig into and rip open baobab trees to gain access to the water inside them. Additionally, elephants use their tusks to bore holes into dry riverbeds to get water hidden underneath the ground.

Sample Answer

Listening Note

Savannah = wide-open grasslands, few trees, and dry seasons

1 **migrate to food and water**
   - Serengeti → hugged herds of migrating animals
   - millions of animals travel 800km → find grasslands and water

2 **elephants**
   - finds water in baobab tree → rip open with tusks and trunks
   - bore holes in dry riverbeds → find water

Sample Response

The professor lectures to the students about how animals have adapted to live in savannahs. He mentions that savannahs are known for having wet and dry seasons. During the dry seasons, there is often little water for animals to drink. As a result, some animals have adapted by migrating to other places in search of water. The professor talks about the great migration that takes place in the Serengeti in Tanzania and Kenya in Africa every year. Millions of animals migrate 800 kilometers in search of water, and then, a few months later, they migrate again when there's a change in the weather. The next example the professor provides is the elephant. The elephant uses its tusks and trunk to access water. It can rip open the baobab tree, which stores large amounts of water, with its tusks and trunk. And it can dig holes in riverbeds to get water beneath the surface.

Actual Test 15

Question 1

p. 93

Sample Answer 1

Today

1 **ingredients listed on all foods**
   - mother reads labels carefully
   - doesn't buy harmful items

2 **many places to buy food**
   - can get good food at different stores
   - make selective purchases

Sample Response

It's much easier for people to eat healthy food today than it was fifty years ago. Nowadays, when you go to the supermarket, you can see the ingredients on everything you buy and can see how nutritious the foods really are. Fifty years ago, that wasn't possible. When I go shopping with my mother, she always makes sure to read the labels carefully. That way, she doesn't feed my family anything that might harm us. There are also numerous places to buy food these days, which makes eating healthy food simple. For instance, we can purchase organic fruits and vegetables at one store and get grain-fed beef at another. By making selective purchases at various stores, we can put nothing but healthy food into our bodies.

Sample Answer 2

Fifty Years Ago

1 food choices 50 years ago were simple
  - few preserved foods, junk foods, and fast foods
  - people ate fresh food

2 people grew up on farms
  - grew or raised own food
  - grandparents ate only healthy food

Sample Response

Fifty years ago, it was much easier for people to eat healthy food than it is today. For one thing, fifty years ago, the food choices available to people were rather simple. There were few preserved foods and very few junk foods and fast foods. Instead, people ate all kinds of fresh foods, which were healthy for them. Another reason is that many people in my country lived on farms fifty years ago. As a result, they grew or raised their own food. My grandparents grew up on farms, and they ate nothing but healthy food. They are astonished by how unhealthy the food most people consume today is. They always comment about how much more nutritious the food they ate growing up was.

Question 2

p. 94

Listening Script

Now listen to two students discussing the announcement.

M Student: I'm so upset right now. I can't believe the school is doing this.

W Student: What are you mad about, Jeff?

M: Bicycles are banned on campus starting next week. Now how am I supposed to get around campus?

W: Personally, I don't have a problem with this ruling. Most of the bicyclists on campus seem to take pride in behaving poorly. For instance, I've nearly been hit by bicyclists twice this week alone.

M: Sure, there are some bicyclists who lack interest in safe behavior, but the majority of us obey traffic laws and don't ride on sidewalks. The school is simply punishing everyone for the behavior of a tiny minority.

W: I don't think so, Jeff. Really, the bicyclists here behave horribly.

M: Okay, but, uh . . . how am I supposed to get from class to class now? This campus is huge.

W: The solution is simple. Take the campus shuttle bus like I do.

M: There aren't enough buses. And they're always packed with students, so you can't get a seat. I guess I'll have to walk to class now. This is so unfair.

Sample Answer

Reading Note

Bicycles banned on campus
- accidents w/bikes & cars → bicyclists' fault
- bicyclists don't follow safety rules

Listening Note

Man → disagrees with ruling

1 most bicyclists obey traffic laws
  - some don't
  - school punishing all because of minority

2 shuttle buses aren't good
  - aren't enough buses
  - can't get a seat
  - will have to walk to class

Sample Response

The man is very upset about the announcement by the dean of students and indicates that he strongly disagrees with it. According to the dean of students, nobody is permitted to ride a bicycle on campus anymore. One reason is that there have been several accidents involving bicyclists, and the bicyclists were at fault in each instance. Another is that bicyclists on campus engage in reckless behavior regarding pedestrians. The man protests this by stating that most bicyclists on campus ride safely and follow the traffic laws. He claims that every bicyclist is getting punished for the poor behavior of a few people. The man further protests the decision because he rides his bike to class. He says he can't take the shuttle bus because it's always full of students. He complains that the campus is too big, so he doesn't want to have to walk to class.

Question 3

p. 95

Listening Script

Now listen to a lecture on this topic in a psychology class.

M Professor: Making quick choices is almost never easy, especially if there are several things going on at once. Permit me, um, permit me to give you a personal example of that.

This summer, I was driving on the interstate with my family. I had turned on my car's navigation system because we were visiting a place I'd never been to before. Anyway, the navigation system suddenly told me I needed to take the upcoming exit. However, according to the road signs, that exit would take me back to the city. I had also looked at a map before we had departed, and I was pretty sure I wanted to take a different exit.

So, uh, the annoying voice on the navigation system kept

telling me to exit the interstate. Then, my wife and kids started telling me to change lanes so that I could take the upcoming exit. I responded by saying they were wrong and insisted we needed a different exit. That started an argument with everyone. Well, I was driving quickly, and everyone, including the machine, was talking. Suddenly, the car in front of us slowed down, and I nearly rammed it. I had to swerve out of the way and, in the process, missed the turnoff. What had happened was that I was suffering from information overload and couldn't make a decision.

Sample Answer

Reading Note

Information Overload

too much info → overwhelms person = stress
info overload = choose 1 of many options quickly
brain can't process info → hard to make right choice

Listening Note

Making quick choices → not easy

driving on interstate w/family

- navigation system said to get off
- professor thought needs other exit

information overload

- navigation system was talking
- wife, children, and professor were arguing
- car in front slowed down → almost hit
- swerved → missed turnoff

Sample Response

As he lectures, the professor tells the students about an incident involving him and his family. He was driving on the interstate once when the navigation system told him to take an exit. But the signs indicated he wanted a different exit, so he was confused. He got in an argument with his wife and children about which exit to take, and then the car in front of him slowed down all of a sudden. He moved into another lane to avoid the car, which caused him to miss the exit. Because of everything going on at the same time, the professor was suffering from information overload. This is a problem which people in the present day have to deal with because of modern technology. When someone suffers from information overload, there's too much information available, so the person has a hard time making a decision, especially if the choice needs to be made quickly.

Question 4   p. 96

Listening Script

Listen to part of a lecture in a zoology class.

W Professor: When it's time to breed, most birds build some sort of nest. Birds use their nests to lay eggs in and then to serve as places to raise their newborn chicks. However, um, both the eggs and nests can be vulnerable to predators, so adult birds must construct their nests in ways that provide some manner of protection.

One way birds do this is to build their nests in places that are either, uh, hard to reach or hard to see. They do this in a variety of ways . . . Most birds simply build nests high above the ground—often in trees—so that ground predators cannot get to their eggs and chicks. These nests are typically constructed from vegetation, so the nests blend into the background, making them difficult to spot. Other birds build nests inside the hollows of trees or on cliff faces or other natural openings. For example, the tropical hornbill makes its nest in a hole in a tree or in a crevice in a cliff. Then, the bird builds a mud wall with a small opening over the entrance to help hide the nest.

Other birds utilize defensive barriers. For instance, uh, they may build their nests with thorny plant matter or make them in thorn thickets to deter predators. Another defensive measure is smell. Some birds use scat, uh, you know, animal feces, when building their nests since the smell drives off predators. The common waxbill, a type of African finch, frequently builds its nest with scat. Research has shown that waxbill nests with scat in them enable more chicks and eggs to survive than nests without any scat.

Sample Answer

Listening Note

Bird nests → lay eggs in and raise newborn chicks

1 **build in places hard to reach or see**
    - trees → high off the ground = safe from ground predators
    - made with vegetation → hard to see
    - nests in hollows of trees or cliff faces → tropical hornbill

2 **defensive barriers**
    - build nests with thorns or in thorn thickets
    - smell → use scat = common waxbill

Sample Response

The professor tells the class that bird nests can be vulnerable to predators, so birds use certain methods when they construct their nests to make them safer. The first thing the professor talks about concerns the location of the nest. The professor states that many birds protect themselves from ground predators by building their nests high above the ground in trees. She also says that other birds build nests in holes in trees or in cliffs. She mentions the tropical hornbill, which makes a mud barrier around its nest to keep predators away. Next, the professor mentions that some birds use defensive barriers when building their nests. For instance, they may make their nests with thorns or even build them in thorn thickets. She comments that some birds use scat when building their nests since it can help repel various animals. In those ways, birds can get some measure of safety from predators.

Actual Test 16

Question 1

p. 99

Sample Answer 1

Go on a Guided Tour

1 **professional tour guide = see important sights**
   - took tour of London
   - saw most famous spots

2 **can't speak language in foreign country**
   - travel with group
   - reduce possibility of problems

Sample Response

Of the three choices, it is my opinion that going on a tour of the city with a small group of people would be the best one. To begin with, by using a professional tour guide, I will get to see all of the important sights in the city. Last year, I took a tour of London, and I was able to see most of the famous spots in the city. For me, that was a great trip. In addition, if I am in a foreign country, I probably cannot speak the language there well. So it would be better for me to travel with a group of people. This would reduce the possibility of having problems due to the language barrier.

Sample Answer 2

Ask a Local Resident

1 **local residents know where to visit**
   - went to Beijing
   - local told me about famous sights

2 **visited museums and marketplaces**
   - most foreign travelers don't see
   - locals can provide helpful information

Sample Response

All three choices are appealing, but I would opt to ask a local resident for advice and then go where that person tells me to. For one thing, local residents know all of the popular

places that people should visit. When I traveled to Beijing one time, a Chinese person who lived there told me which of the famous sights I needed to see. In addition, she told me about a few places that most tourists don't know about. That's another advantage of talking to a local resident. I got to visit a couple of fascinating museums and marketplaces that most foreign travelers never get to see. Only local residents are capable of providing that kind of helpful information.

Question 2

p. 100

Listening Script

Now listen to two students discussing the announcement.

M Student: Well, this announcement by the student dining services office is a bit interesting. Have you seen it?

W Student: Do you mean the announcement that the cafeterias are going to offer more food choices? Personally, I'm in favor of it because I'm looking forward to trying different types of ethnic food.

M: Yes, but didn't you notice the part about the prices of meal plans increasing?

W: Sure, but it's not a big increase.

M: Maybe not for you, but it is for me. It's already difficult for me to afford to attend school here. With this price increase, I might have to take out a loan next semester.

W: I'm really sorry to hear that, Stuart.

M: However, there's something that I like about this announcement.

W: What's that?

M: Where I grew up, I never got the opportunity to try a wide variety of food. I mean, uh, my parents basically cooked the same few meals all the time. So I've never had the opportunity to sample much ethnic food. I'm really looking forward to trying out some food from different countries, especially those in Asia.

W: Yeah, I agree with you. I simply love Russian and Indian food and can't wait to get to eat them regularly.

Sample Answer

Reading Note

Ethnic food to be served at cafeterias

- food from Japan, India, Russia, and other countries
- meal plan price = 15% increase
- all students in dorms must purchase meal plan

Listening Note

Man → has mixed feelings

1 **dislikes meal plan price increase**

- has difficulty affording school
- may need to take out loan

2 **likes variety of food**
   - ate same food growing up
   - wants to sample ethnic food
   - especially wants to try Asian food

The two students are having a conversation about an announcement by the student dining services office. According to the announcement, all of the school's dining halls are going to begin serving various types of ethnic food in the coming semester. It also mentions that because more food options are being provided to students, the price of each meal plan is going to increase by fifteen percent. The man has mixed feelings about the announcement. To begin with, he comments that he is having trouble paying his tuition. Now, because of the change, he will have to pay more money for a meal plan, and he doesn't believe he can afford it. On the other hand, the man really wants to try food from other countries. He indicates that he didn't get a chance to do that at his home, so now he is looking forward to sample new types of food.

Question 3 p. 101

Listening Script

Now listen to a lecture on this topic in a zoology class.

M Professor: In hot deserts such as the Sahara, most animals hide during the midday heat, but that's not true for all of them. In fact, some animals have a high tolerance for heat.

One is the Saharan silver ant. This ant has special hairs on the top and sides of its body which create a, uh, a heat shield. The hairs make the ant appear to be silver in color, hence its name. Basically, they reflect solar radiation and also help the ant dissipate the body heat it absorbs in the desert. An additional feature is that the ant lacks hair on its underside, which keeps its body away from the hot desert floor. Thanks to these features, the Saharan silver ant is active during the day, when it hunts for food.

Another thermophile that lives in the Sahara Desert and is active during daylight hours is the desert monitor lizard. Growing up to two meters in length, it can tolerate extremely hot temperatures thanks to its skin. It is tough enough to prevent the lizard from overheating as it can repel heat from the sun. The lizard also has salt glands, which enable it to avoid losing water from its body. Those two adaptations are what let it hunt when other creatures must hide from the heat.

Reading Note

Thermophiles = live in extremely hot conditions

- high tolerance for heat → can survive in hostile environments
- live in hot deserts, undersea thermal vents, & insides of volcanoes

Listening Note

Some desert animals → high tolerance for heat

1 **Saharan silver ant**
   - hairs on body → make heat shield
   - reflect solar radiation → dissipate body heat
   - no hair on underside = keeps body away from desert floor

2 **desert monitor lizard**
   - tough skin repels sun's heat
   - salt glands → keep it from losing water from body

The professor lectures to the students about two animals, the Saharan silver ant and the desert monitor lizard. According to him, both have a high tolerance for heat. The Saharan silver ant has hairs on the upper part of its body that create a heat shield which can deflect the sun's heat. The ant additionally lacks hair on its underside, so its body is farther away from the desert floor. Thanks to those two features, the ant can be active during the day. As for the desert monitor lizard, it has skin that can keep the sun from overheating the lizard. It has salt glands that help the lizard preserve water in its body, too. Thanks to those parts of its body, the lizard is a daytime hunter. Both of these animals are thermophiles. These are animals that can not only live in hot temperatures but can also thrive in these conditions.

Question 4 p. 102

Listening Script

Listen to part of a lecture in a business class.

W Professor: You know, uh, these days, it's easier than ever for companies to sell the products they manufacture directly to customers. Instead of relying upon retail stores to sell the majority of their goods, these companies establish online shops and sell their own products. If you ask me, that's a rather clever thing to do.

One of the reasons is that manufacturers are able to sell their products for lower prices than retail stores. After all, they don't have to deal with overhead such as rent on a building and the wages of the sales staff. And even though the sale prices are lower, manufacturers can still enjoy healthy profit margins. Lower prices naturally attract more customers, so manufacturers can improve their sales numbers, too. Nowadays, thanks to the Internet, many manufacturers have increased their revenues and profits due to direct online sales.

Additionally, how many times have you gone to a retail store and seen damaged or broken items for sale or items that were less than perfect? Probably a lot, right? And if you inquired as to when new items in better condition would be arriving, you were most likely told you'd have to wait a week or two for a shipment to get there. Yeah, I can't stand when that happens either. Well, customers know that if they buy directly from manufacturers, they won't be receiving any faulty items. After all, uh, manufacturers can instantly replace broken or damaged items with ones in perfect condition. Therefore, um, customers won't have to wait for new items to arrive like they would if they were shopping at physical stores.

Sample Answer

Listening Note

Companies sell goods online = clever

1 **can sell for lower prices than retail stores**
   - no overhead
   - low prices but healthy profit margins
   - can attract more customers

2 **no faulty items sold online**
   - don't have to wait for stores to order more
   - can instantly get items in perfect condition

Sample Response

The professor lectures to the students about the benefits of companies selling their own products directly to customers. She makes two points that support her argument in favor of doing so. The first is that manufacturers can gain more customers because they're able to sell their goods for prices lower than those at retail stores. The professor points out that manufacturers will make a profit even with lower prices because they do not have to worry about overhead such as rent and employee salaries. The second point that she makes concerns items which are damaged or in poor condition. She notes that when stores have low-quality items on sale, customers might need to wait a while for new items to be ordered and to arrive. However, by purchasing directly from manufacturers, customers can be assured that they won't be getting anything faulty.

Actual Test 17

Question 1

p. 105

Sample Answer 1

An Apartment Downtown

1 **love big cities**
   - work in central part, so home is close to workplace
   - excellent restaurants, cafés, and shopping places

2 **don't need big home**
   - live alone
   - have small place now

Sample Response

If I had to select one of the two residences, I would choose the small apartment located in the middle of downtown. The first reason is that I love big cities and would have a great time living downtown. I work in the central part of my city, so my home would therefore be close to my workplace. There would also be lots of excellent restaurants, cafés, and shopping places for me to visit in my free time. The second reason is that I don't need a big home. I live alone, so I don't require a home with many rooms. In fact, my current place only has a kitchen, a bedroom, and a bathroom, and that's as much space as I need at this time.

Sample Answer 2

A House in the Suburbs

1 **great public transportation**
   - take bus or subway to work and home
   - read books, listen to music, or relax

2 **home now is cramped**
   - want bigger house
   - enough room for possessions
   - can have yard

Sample Response

I would definitely prefer living in a house in the suburbs to an apartment downtown. First, even though the house would be far from my workplace, that wouldn't bother me too much. My city has great public transportation, so I could take the bus or the subway to work and home every day. While I commute, I would read books, listen to music, or relax. Second, I presently live in a small place that's very cramped, so I would enjoy having a bigger house. I could have plenty of room for all of my furniture, books, and other items. In addition, if I lived in the suburbs, I would likely have a yard, which is something that I have always wanted.

Question 2

p. 106

Listening Script

Now listen to two students discussing the announcement.

M Student: Hmm . . . I'm not sure what to think of the announcement that the commuter rail is going to run all the way to campus.

W Student: I know exactly how I feel. I'm totally against it.

M: Yeah? But don't you live downtown? Won't this be a great way for you to get to school?

W: Probably, but I already take the bus to campus. It gets me to school fast, and I don't have to pay much to take it. I don't think the school needs a commuter line since students like me who live downtown can take buses instead.

M: I suppose. But the train will be faster than the bus since it won't get caught in any traffic jams.

W: That's true, but think about the construction.

M: Huh? What do you mean?

W: According to the announcement, it's going to require practically an entire year to build both the station and the railway line. That construction work is going to happen in the middle of each semester.

M: So what?

W: Brian, think about it. How much noise is the construction going to cause? I've got classes in Benedict Hall, and so do you. It's going to be difficult to hear our professors lecture, and imagine trying to concentrate while taking a test with all that noise going on.

Sample Answer

Reading Note

Construction on train station and railway line on campus

- will connect to commuter line
- will take 11 months to finish
- will transport students from downtown → fast & cheap

Listening Note

Woman → against construction

1 **takes bus to school**
   - fast and cheap
   - school doesn't need commuter line

2 **long construction period**
   - will happen in middle of 2 semesters
   - lots of noise
   - hard to hear professors + can't concentrate during tests

Sample Response

The students discuss an announcement by the university development office. It is about a train station and a

railway line that will be built to connect the school with the downtown area. The announcement claims that it will take eleven months to make, and upon completion, students will be able to travel on it cheaply and quickly. The woman tells the man that she is against the building of the railway line. She has two reasons for being against it. First, she tells the man that she lives downtown and takes the bus to school. She remarks that it is a fast and cheap method of getting to school. Second, she is concerned about the noise that will be caused by the construction workers during the semester. She doesn't want to be bothered by the noise while professors are lecturing and she is taking exams.

Question 3

p. 107

Listening Script

Now listen to a lecture on this topic in a psychology class.

W Professor: Okay, uh, now I'd like to give you a personal example of the holiday paradox so that you can see how it actually works. Let me tell you about the trip that I took with my husband during last summer vacation.

We visited the southern part of France for three weeks during July and August. Neither of us had ever traveled there before, so we were quite eager to see as much as we could. Just about every day, we visited someplace new. For instance, we traveled to old medieval villages, toured castles, went to numerous museums and art galleries, and spent some time swimming in the Mediterranean Sea as well. We were having so much fun that the day before we were scheduled to return home, we were stunned upon realizing that our trip was near its end. I guess the old saying is true: Time flies when you're having fun.

Well, uh, we flew back home, and a week later, it seemed to me that we had been in France for nearly the entire summer. I felt as though we'd been there for three months, not three weeks. Why's that? Well, we made so many new memories that our time there appeared to have been longer than it really was.

Sample Answer

Reading Note

The Holiday Paradox

people travel & have fun → time moves quickly
holiday ends → created new memories → vacation seems longer than was in reality

Listening Note

Professor and husband → trip to France

1 **wanted to see everything**
   - visited new places daily

- did many activities
- realized had to go home next day = stunned → time flew by

2 went back home
- seemed like had been in France for three months, not three weeks
- made many new memories → time appeared longer than really was

Sample Response

The professor shares a personal story with the students about a trip that she took with her husband last summer. She and her husband visited France, which she had never gone to before. They did all kinds of sightseeing activities while they were on their trip, and they had a great time on their three-week vacation. She comments that she and her husband were surprised by how fast time had seemed to have passed when their trip was over. However, she then points out that a week later, it appeared to her as if her trip had been much longer than three weeks. This feeling is related to the holiday paradox. According to it, people having fun think time passes quickly. But since they create so many new memories in a short period of time, they get the impression that their trip lasted longer than it did in reality.

Question 4

p. 108

Listening Script

Listen to part of a lecture in a marketing class.

M Professor: Because companies can sell goods on the global market, they frequently look to make money in foreign countries. But most businesses lack the infrastructure to sell goods abroad. As a result, many turn to licensing their products to foreign companies. In case you don't know, when a company licenses a product, it gives another firm permission to use its product somehow. The product could be a manufactured good, a book, medicine, uh, just about anything . . . The company receiving the license is normally allowed to make the product and can then sell it.

Sounds good, right? Well . . . licensing can increase a company's short-term profits but may have some long-term disadvantages. One is that companies cannot usually control the quality of the products being made by other firms. For instance, a few years ago, a bicycle manufacturer here sold a license to a firm in South America. It had created a new aerodynamic design for bikes that was outstanding. However, the South American company used inferior materials, so the bikes were of poor quality. That damaged the reputation of the company which had sold the license.

Additionally, when companies sell licenses to foreign firms,

they can wind up competing with those companies in the future. If a new technology is created, the company selling the license must teach the foreign company how to use it. This provides the foreign company with more knowledge than it had possessed previously. The company may use this technology transfer to create products of its own later. Thus, um, the company that sells the license may successfully sell its products abroad for a while, but it stands a good chance of being pushed out of the market by its foreign partners later.

Sample Answer

Listening Note

Firms sell licenses to companies abroad = long-term disadvantages

1 can't control quality of product
- bicycle maker sold license to foreign firm
- inferior materials used → bikes were of poor quality
- original company's reputation damaged

2 companies selling licenses may compete w/firms in future
- must teach licensing firm how to use technology
- gives firm more knowledge
- can create its own products w/technology
- then competes w/company that sells license

Sample Response

In his lecture, the professor discusses some disadvantages to companies that sell licenses of their products to foreign businesses. The professor first explains that selling a license entitles another firm to make and sell a product. The first disadvantage he discusses is that the firm that sells the license can't control how well the other company manufactures its product. He mentions a firm that sold a license to another one to make bicycles. Unfortunately, the licensing company made the bikes poorly, and that damaged the first company's reputation. The second disadvantage the professor talks about concerns technology transfers. These happen when a company must teach the licensing firm how to make a product. The licensing firm can use this knowledge later to make its own products that directly compete with the original company. So the firm that made the product could lose out in the foreign market later.

Actual Test 18

Question 1 p. 111

Sample Answer 1

New Textbooks

1 **advantages**
- taking notes = easy
- new books updated more often → have current knowledge

2 **disadvantages**
- expensive → can't afford
- only minor changes in updated versions

Sample Response

New textbooks definitely have both advantages and disadvantages. I'll cover the advantages of them first. I like taking notes in the margins of books, and I can do that easily when I have a new, clean textbook. In addition, I purchase lots of science textbooks, which constantly get updated because of discoveries being made. As a result, by purchasing new textbooks, I can be assured of having the latest editions, which will be updated with current knowledge. However, new textbooks are pretty expensive, so many students who don't work part time have trouble affording them. Additionally, most of the newest editions have just minor changes, so there is really no need for most students to buy updated versions of textbooks.

Sample Answer 2

Used Textbooks

1 **advantages**
- cost less than new ones
- important passages marked → helpful to new owners

2 **disadvantages**
- pages missing + text marked on = hard to read
- old editions → outdated or incorrect information

Sample Response

Personally, I love used textbooks and feel that they have numerous advantages. The primary one is that used textbooks cost less than new ones. That's a huge benefit to students like me who don't have jobs and aren't wealthy. In addition, previous owners often mark up the important passages in their textbooks, so their highlights and comments can be helpful to later owners of used textbooks. On the other hand, some prior owners don't take care of their books, so used books may have pages missing or text that has been marked on, making it hard to read. Used

textbooks may also be old editions containing outdated or incorrect information, which is another big disadvantage to people who buy them.

Question 2 p. 112

Listening Script

Now listen to two students discussing the letter.

W Student: The person who wrote this letter to the editor is so right. The school shouldn't be increasing the price of a parking pass again.

M Student: I don't care since I don't have a car and live on campus. But out of curiosity, why do you feel that way?

W: It's simple really. First, this is just a money grab by the school. I mean, uh, the price of a parking pass is going up by twenty percent.

M: Is that a lot?

W: It's an enormous increase. The previous two increases were only five and eight percent, respectively. This one is much bigger.

M: I wonder why. Maybe the school needs funding to build a new parking lot or to, um, to improve the parking infrastructure.

W: I wish. In fact, if the school were going to use the money to make the parking situation here better, I think most students wouldn't be upset. As it is, on-campus parking is hard to find, and the school isn't doing anything to change the situation.

M: What's the extra money going to be used for?

W: I've heard that it will go into the school's general fund. So it's not being earmarked for anything to do with parking.

M: That doesn't seem right.

Sample Answer

Reading Note

Parking pass price = going up

- third consecutive year of increases
- unfair to students
- no public transportation → students off campus must drive

Listening Note

Woman → agrees w/letter writer

1 **money grab**
- price going up by 20%
- previous increases were small

2 **money not used for parking infrastructure**
- hard to find on-campus parking

- money goes to school's general fund

The woman talks to the man about a letter to the editor that a student sent to the school newspaper. The letter writer is displeased with the fact that the school is planning to increase the price of a parking pass for students. She points out that due to the lack of public transportation in the area, students living off campus have to drive to the school and must therefore pay for a parking pass. The woman agrees with the letter writer. She is upset about the price hike because it is much bigger than the increases during the previous two years. In fact, the woman calls it a money grab by the school. She also expresses her disappointment that the school won't use the money to make parking on campus better. Instead, the money will go into the school's general fund, which makes her very unhappy.

Question 3

p. 113

Listening Script

Now listen to a lecture on this topic in a marketing class.

M Professor: Take a look at this item I'm holding in my hand. Now, uh, don't laugh. I know most of you don't use cameras which require film these days but instead rely on your mobile devices to take pictures. However, it wasn't so long ago that people were using cameras like this one all the time.

Anyway, I believe this camera can provide a perfect example of what value analysis is. See, uh, around twenty years ago, this camera was one of the top-selling models in the world. The firm that manufactured it did a great job and made an outstanding piece of equipment. The company even sold it with a beautiful leather case.

However, uh, the problem was that the firm wasn't making enough money from the camera, so it wasn't very profitable. It then conducted some market research on the customers who had bought it, and it was surprised by one of the most common comments. Apparently, the customers simply weren't interested in the leather case. They just wanted the camera and didn't care about anything fancy. Well, the company replaced the leather case with a much cheaper nylon one. Then, it reduced the price but still managed to increase its profits. The camera ultimately became even more popular and made the company tons of money.

Sample Answer

Reading Note

Value Analysis

companies want to reduce costs of projects

- determine functions
- search for inexpensive ways to provide functions
- need to maintain quality and customer satisfaction
- high profit margin

Listening Note

Old film camera

1 **was one of top-selling models**
   - great piece of equipment
   - came w/leather case

2 **firm didn't make enough money**
   - did market research
   - customers didn't care about case → just wanted camera
   - replaced leather case w/nylon one
   - price went down, but profits went up

The professor shows the students his camera, which is one from the past that uses film. He tells the class that the camera was a bestselling model about two decades ago. He also states that the manufacturer felt that it wasn't making enough money from the camera, so it did some market research to figure out what to do. Among the feedback it received was that the customers had no interest in the leather case. The company then replaced the case with a nylon one, which lowered the price of the camera yet improved its profit margin. This action made the company lots of money. The action was also a case of value analysis. This happens when companies try to figure out the cheapest way to make products that function well and satisfy their customers. In doing so, businesses can improve their profits on the products they make.

Question 4

p. 114

Listening Script

Listen to part of a lecture in a zoology class.

M Professor: Now, uh, you've probably noticed in the textbook that when it gives descriptions of animals, it provides their average sizes and weights. For instance, it notes that a male gray wolf stands between 1.4 and 1.8 meters high while weighing between forty-three and forty-five kilograms. But, well, keep in mind that those are just averages. And humans can, interestingly, influence the sizes of many animals.

We have a thriving whitetail deer population in the surrounding area. The deer look big, don't they . . . ? Well, actually, most local whitetail deer are quite small, and there's a reason for that . . . It's hunting. Now, uh, don't misunderstand. Hunting deer doesn't make them small. On the contrary, it reduces the local population, so there's more food for the remaining deer, so they tend to grow bigger. But there's been a ban on deer hunting here for five years, so the population has exploded. There's not enough food for them though, so they aren't growing to normal sizes. In fact, they're way too small.

The opposite is also true. By that, I mean that humans can cause animals which are normally small to become much larger than normal. Rats are a perfect example. In the past, rats didn't grow to very large sizes, but go downtown tonight and look around, and you'll see some enormous rats. The reason is that humans have created ideal conditions for rats. Think about it . . . We throw out tons of food and other garbage that rats eat. We construct buildings with plenty of places for them to make nests in. And we remove animals such as stray dogs and cats that hunt them. Thanks to humans, rats have increased in size over time.

Sample Answer

Listening Note

Human actions → affect sizes of animals

1 **whitetail deer**
   - local deer small → no hunting
   - population has gone up
   - not enough food → aren't growing to normal sizes

2 **rats**
   - ideal conditions for them → food, buildings, no stray animals
   - created conditions for rats to get big

Sample Response

During his lecture, the professor talks about the sizes of animals. He remarks that it is possible for humans to affect how big or small some animals become. He uses whitetail deer and rats as examples of this. First, he discusses the whitetail deer. He tells the students that the local whitetail deer are much smaller than average. He says that a ban on deer hunting for the past five years has caused the deer population in the area to increase greatly. However, the deer aren't getting enough food to eat, so they are not growing very large. Next, the professor discusses rats. According to him, rats have become very big in recent times because of humans. Humans produce food that rats eat, provide places where they can live, and remove animals that hunt rats. These three actions have allowed rats to increase in size.

Actual Test 19

Question 1 p. 117

Sample Answer 1

Reading Club

1 **huge reader**
   - read 2-4 books/week
   - no problem to read 1 book for club

2 **love discussing books**
   - can be surrounded by book lovers
   - might make new friends

Sample Response

Considering the three choices, I am confident in selecting the book club as the one I would prefer to join. The main reason is that I'm a huge reader. I actually read between two and four books each week, so being required to read one book for the book club every week would not be a problem for me. A secondary reason is that not only do I love reading, but I also love discussing books with others. Most of my friends don't read much, but if I joined a book club, I'd be surrounded by book lovers. We could discuss the nuances of books, and I might even make a few good friends in the club since we would have something in common.

Sample Answer 2

Hiking Club

1 **enjoy nature**
   - walk in forests and mountains near home
   - fresh air, wild animals, and scenery

2 **am overweight**
   - need to exercise to lose weight
   - hiking = rigorous exercise

Sample Response

If I had to choose between a reading club, a hiking club, and a movie club, I'd join the hiking club. There are two reasons I'd do that. The first is that I enjoy spending time in nature. As a member of a hiking club, I'd get the opportunity to walk in the area near my home. There are forests and mountains here, so the club members would surely walk through them. I could breathe fresh air, see wild animals, and enjoy the scenery. Next, I'm overweight and need to exercise to lose weight and to get in shape. By joining a hiking club, I'd do some rigorous exercise at least once a week, and that's something I definitely need to do.

Question 2

p. 118

Listening Script

Now listen to two students discussing the announcement.

M Student: What a great idea. I'm glad the administration finally listened to some of us and agreed to open an online market for used books.

W Student: Oh, were you one of the people who spoke to Dean Watson about doing that?

M: I sure was. This is something we desperately need since the manager at the school bookstore refuses to purchase used books from students.

W: Yeah, that's right.

M: You know, this semester, several of my books cost more than one hundred dollars apiece. It will be great to be able to get some of my money back by selling them to underclassmen.

W: Why are your books so expensive?

M: I'm taking an art history class and a physics class, and books in those fields are often ridiculously expensive.

W: I had no idea. So what did you do with your textbooks in the past?

M: I didn't want to throw them away, so I just kept them in my dorm rooms. Now I've got a huge pile of books in my room, and they're really making it cramped. I hope I can sell most of them. Then, I'll both make some money and get more space in my room.

W: Good luck.

Sample Answer

Reading Note

School will run online used book market

- all students can sell and buy books
- must use student ID number
- students responsible for quality and prices of books

Listening Note

Man → glad about decision

1 **spent lots of money on books**
   - wants to sell to get money back
   - school bookstore won't buy used books

2 **kept books from previous classes**
   - big pile on dorm room floor = cramped room
   - wants to sell most books
   - make money + get more space

Sample Response

The man and the woman discuss an announcement made by the school administration. It reads that the school will operate an online market where students can buy and sell used textbooks. The man is pleased with the school's decision. In fact, he indicates to the woman that he is partially responsible for the school's decision to open the online market. The man has two reasons for being happy about the new market. The first is that he wants to get back some of the money he spent on books this semester. He remarks that some of his books are very expensive, and since he can't sell them to the university bookstore, he intends to sell them online. Next, the man says that he has kept all of the books that he purchased for previous classes. They are taking up space in his dorm room, so he wants to sell some to free up some room.

Question 3

p. 119

Listening Script

Now listen to a lecture on this topic in an education class.

W Professor: Most of you probably don't know this, but many years ago, I used to be a kindergarten teacher. Like all teaching, there were various challenges that I had to overcome to become a good instructor. I'd like to tell you about one of these challenges.

One of the students' favorite activities was cutting paper with scissors. Basically, they would fold paper and then cut various shapes. Making animal shapes was easily one of the students' favorite activities year in and year out. Unfortunately, in order to cut these shapes out, the students had to make several different cuts in the paper.

So, um, as you can imagine, this resulted in problems because some students were able to finish faster than others. Sadly, some of these students teased the slower students, which made them feel bad. So here's what I did . . . I provided help to the slower students and taught them how to complete each task one at a time. At the same time, I added extra tasks for the faster students. I made the faster students paste the animal figures to paper and then had them color the animals. That kept the fast students busy, so the teasing stopped, and I was able to provide individual assistance—you know, hurdle help—to the students who needed it.

Sample Answer

Reading Note

Hurdle Help

children face obstacles when doing tasks
- may need several steps
- step = like hurdle in track and field
- teacher provides assistance = child can complete task

Listening Note

Had challenge as kindergarten teacher

1 **students liked cutting animal shapes w/scissors**
   - fold paper → cut into shapes
   - had to make several cuts in paper

2 **some students finished faster than others**
   - had to provide help to slower students
   - showed them how to do tasks one at a time = hurdle help

Sample Response

The professor talks about the time when she was a kindergarten teacher. She remarks that her students often enjoyed cutting out paper into the shapes of different animals. However, to accomplish this task, the students had to make several different cuts. Because some students were faster than the others and then teased the slower students, the professor felt like she needed to provide extra instruction for the slow students. So she gave the fast students some tasks to occupy themselves. Then, she took the time to work together with the slow students to provide them with individual instruction. She showed them how to cut out the animals one step at a time. What the professor did was hurdle help. This happens when a person provides instruction on how to complete a task that requires multiple steps. Each step is like a hurdle that has to be leaped over.

Question 4   p. 120

Listening Script

Listen to part of a lecture in a zoology class.

W Professor: Please take a look at the next slide . . . This is a termite nest. Notice how high above the ground it rises. Depending upon the species, the nests in which colonies of termites live can rise more than a couple of meters above the ground or descend extremely far beneath it. I know you're all aware of the destructive nature of termites, but their nests can actually provide some benefits to the local ecosystem.

Take a look at this picture . . . and this one . . . Notice how in both pictures, there's an animal at the top of the termite nest. All kinds of animals, including numerous species of birds as well as various mammals and reptiles, do this. Now, um, you may be wondering how these animals are benefiting merely by standing on the nests. Well, in many areas, termite nests are the highest objects. Animals therefore use them as sort of, uh, observation posts. By climbing to the top, they can survey the surrounding area. That enables these animals to find food as well as to identify predators, which, uh, which lets them avoid becoming food.

Here's something else . . . Many species of termites, such as the Formosan termite, build nests underground. Some Formosan termite nests can be nearly 100 meters long. What happens is that this softens the ground a great deal. As a result, when rain falls, much more water than normal gets absorbed by the ground, which increases the groundwater supply. This can have a tremendous effect on the local ecology. In some cases, deserts or semiarid regions have literally changed to become green zones full of vegetation thanks to termites.

Sample Answer

Listening Note

Termites = provide benefits to ecosystem

1 **animals on top of termite nests**
   - highest objects in area
   - used as observation posts
   - find food + identify predators

2 **underground nests → Formosan termite**
   - softens ground
   - water gets absorbed when rain → increases groundwater supply
   - converts deserts and semiarid regions to green zones

Sample Response

The professor lectures about termites. While she mentions that they can be destructive, she comments that termites provide a few benefits. She then proceeds to talk about two of them. The first benefit happens when termites build very tall nests above the ground. According to the professor, some termite nests can be more than two meters high. She states that birds, reptiles, and mammals often rest on top of these mounds. By using the nests as observation posts, the animals can look for both food and predators. The next point the professor makes involves the Formosan termite, which builds underground nests. She notes that some of these nests can be 100 meters in length. The nests help make the ground soft and thereby increase its ability to absorb rainwater. This can help make dry regions green areas, so termite nests can cause big changes in local ecosystems.

Actual Test 20

Question 1
p. 123

Group Project

1 **like collaborating w/others**
   - worked w/classmates in past
   - enjoyed + learned

2 **focus on one aspect**
   - can learn something in depth
   - increase chances of doing good work = good grade

Sample Response

Given a choice between doing a group project and writing a twenty-page paper, I would select the group project for sure. One of the reasons is that I enjoy collaborating with others on projects, and doing this kind of a project would let me work together with some of my classmates. In the past, when I did group projects, I not only enjoyed myself but also learned in the process. Another reason is that I would get a chance to focus on one aspect of the group project and then work exclusively on it. This would let me learn something in depth and also increase my chances of doing excellent work. That would enable my team to receive a good grade on the project.

Sample Answer 2

Twenty-Page Paper

1 **individualist**
   - don't enjoy working on team
   - lazy members don't work
   - have to do extra work

2 **like research and writing**
   - can write long papers
   - can learn → point of going to school

Sample Response

I can't stand group projects, so I would much rather write a twenty-page paper. I'm an individualist, so working with a team isn't something I enjoy. The majority of people doing group projects do little work and rely on one or two students to complete them. I'm usually one of those people who have to do the extra work, and it bothers me when lazy people don't help out. In addition, I enjoy doing both research and writing, and I'm pretty good at both. I have written long papers before, so writing a twenty-page paper wouldn't be a problem for me. It's also something I could learn from, and that's the point of taking classes and going to school.

Question 2
p. 124

Listening Script

Now listen to two students discussing the announcement.

W Student: Oh, I can hardly wait to use the new tables and chairs being set up at the lake. It's one of the most popular places on campus, you know.

M Student: I'm not as excited as you are. I can see some advantages, but there are some problems, too.

W: Seriously? Personally, I think it will be a great place to study when the library is full. In fact, I'm looking forward to using them soon.

M: I agree with you there. I also love studying at the lake. I've always had to lie down on the grass, which is annoying, so it will be nice to be able to be seated there.

W: Yeah, you're right. We should study there together some time soon.

M: Sure, we can do that. But, uh, let me tell you what I'm concerned about.

W: What is it?

M: The area around the lake already has a ton of garbage around it since people often litter there. Imagine how bad it's going to be if even more students start going there.

W: Oh, yeah. I hadn't considered that.

M: I just hope that the school sets up a bunch of garbage cans in the area. Otherwise, it's going to look terrible, and the lake itself stands a good chance of getting polluted.

Sample Answer

Reading Note

Tables and chairs to be set up at lake

- used by students, faculty, and administration members
- let people study, do research, and socialize
- use on first-come, first-served basis

Listening Note

Man → sees advantages and disadvantages

1 **likes studying at lake**
   - had to lie on grass before
   - can be seated now
   - will study there w/woman

2 **lots of garbage at lake**
   - litter = will increase if more students go
   - hopes garbage cans are set up
   - could look terrible + lake could get polluted

During the conversation with the woman, the man talks about his opinion regarding the announcement by the buildings and grounds division at the school. It indicates that some tables and chairs will be set up around a lake and that students, faculty, and administration members can use them to study at or to do other activities at. The man both dislikes and likes the announcement by the school. First of all, he mentions that he likes studying at the lake. In the past, he had to lie on the grass, but now he will be able to study there while seated. However, the student then points out the huge amount of litter at the lake since many students don't throw away their trash. He comments that he is very concerned about the area getting dirty and the lake becoming polluted.

Question 3

p. 125

Listening Script

Now listen to a lecture on this topic in a psychology class.

M Professor: When I was younger, plenty of people played various role-playing games. Many of these games involved creating characters that might, uh, fight monsters in dungeons, travel to alien worlds, or do other similar activities. They were really fun, and I remember playing several of them during my teenage years.

Well, uh, there was this one role-playing game which became very popular due to some claims that were made about it. According to the makers of the game, people who played it for several months were able to increase their intelligence. There were all sorts of testimonials about the game in advertisements for it. People made comments stating that they had become A students after playing the game or that they had increased their IQs by several points thanks to a few months of gaming.

It sounds great, doesn't it? But guess what . . . It was fake science. Some researchers conducted multiple studies on people who played the game, and they determined that there was absolutely no truth to the claims being made by its makers. Playing that game didn't lead to better grades at school or increased intelligence. Sure, uh, it was a fun game, but it wasn't possible for people to improve intellectually by playing it.

Sample Answer

Reading Note

Pseudoscience = fake science

- makes claims that can't be falsified
- impossible to test
- astrology = type of pseudoscience

- relies on stories and claims by people

Listening Note

Role-playing games = popular during professor's youth

1 **one popular role-playing game**
   - said could increase people's intelligence
   - testimonials by people in ads
   - said had become A students or increased IQs

2 **claims = fake science**
   - researchers conducted studies
   - no truth to claims
   - didn't result in higher grades or increased intelligence

During his lecture, the professor mentions to the students that he used to play some role-playing games when he was a teenager. He talks about one popular game whose makers stated that it could improve the intelligence of the people who played it. According to them, by playing this role-playing game for just a few months, people could transform into A students and improve their IQs by a significant amount. The professor then remarks that some studies were later done on the game, and it was discovered that the claims by its makers used fake science. There was no proof that the game could make people smarter. This is an example of pseudoscience. It relies on claims that can't be falsified, which is an indication that something is not real science. Additionally, pseudoscience uses stories, not actual science, to make statements about something.

Question 4

p. 126

Listening Script

Listen to part of a lecture in a botany class.

W Professor: Take a look at what I have right here in my hands . . . As you can see, I'm holding a variety of seeds. There are, uh, ten different types of seeds to be exact. At present, these seeds are dormant, which means they haven't germinated and aren't developing into new plants. The fact that seeds remain dormant until growing conditions are ideal is a huge benefit to plants. Let me explain why.

First of all, seed dispersal is what allows plants to spread to other areas. Dispersal can happen in many ways, including being carried by birds or other animals, being blown away by the wind, and being moved by water. Because seeds do not germinate immediately but remain dormant until precise conditions are met, dormancy allows them to spread to areas far and wide. As a result, plants are not contained in small areas but can instead be found growing in a wide variety of places. This results in increased diversity in forests.

Secondly, seeds have developed over time to remain dormant until ideal conditions for growing exist. This typically involves a combination of soil, heat, sunlight, and water. For example, most seeds remain dormant in cold conditions. After all, uh, if they were to start growing in winter, most would quickly die because of low temperatures, a lack of sunlight, and snow accumulation. The seeds of some plants can also be extremely picky. Many seeds of plants in Australia, including eucalyptus and acacia trees, won't germinate unless they're exposed to extreme heat. This happens after forest fires. In those cases, the seeds fall into nutrient-rich ash and begin growing, giving them a better chance of survival.

Sample Answer

Listening Note

Seed dormancy = benefits plants

1 **allows for seed dispersal**
   - seeds carried by animals + moved by wind and water
   - don't germinate immediately
   - lets plants spread to new areas → increase diversity in forests

2 **stay dormant until conditions are ideal**
   - need soil, heat, sunlight, and water
   - avoid dying by growing in bad conditions
   - eucalyptus and acacia trees → seeds germinate after forest fires
   - lets them grow in nutrient-rich ash = survival chances higher

Sample Response

The professor talks about seed dormancy in her lecture. Seed dormancy means that seeds don't germinate but instead wait until ideal conditions of soil, water, light, and heat are met. She comments that one benefit of seed dormancy is that it lets seeds be dispersed widely. She notes that birds and other animals, the wind, and the water can transport seeds to other places. Then, seeds can germinate, become plants, and increase the amount of plant diversity in new regions. The second point the professor makes is that seeds benefit by waiting until the conditions needed for them to grow well are right. She remarks that, for instance, seeds don't germinate in winter because they would die from the poor environmental conditions. She also talks about some trees in Australia that don't germinate until after forest fires. This ensures that they have plenty of nutrient-rich soil to grow in.

Memo